THE ADDICTION OF A BUSY LIFE

GW00691410

The Addiction of a Busy Life

Edward England

AVIEMORE BOOKS
CROWBOROUGH, EAST SUSSEX

Scripture quotations are taken from
the Holy Bible, New International Version,
copyright © 1973, 1978, 1984 by the International Bible
Society, and used by permission of Hodder & Stoughton Ltd;
The Revised Standard Version copyrighted 1946, 1952,
© 1971, 1973 by the Division of Christian Education
and Ministry of the National Council of Churches
of Christ in the USA; The Living Bible
© Tyndale House Publishers 1971.

British Library Cataloguing Data
A catalogue record for this book is available
from the British Library.

ISBN 1 901387 09 7

Designed and produced by Bookprint Creative Services
P.O. Box 827, BN21 3YJ, England for
AVIEMORE BOOKS
c/o Christina Press Ltd,
Highland House, Aviemore Road
Crowborough, East Sussex, TN6 1QX.
Printed in Great Britain.

To Ann,
my wife and constant friend,
for being there, as always, in the hour of crisis;
and for permitting me (if a bit reluctantly)
to quote a few extracts from her journal
never intended for publication.

Acknowledgements

I owe special thanks to Rob Parsons for his gracious foreword; to Canon John Gunstone, Tony and Jane Collins, and the Rev. Andrew Cornes for their editorial comments; to Marion Cameron for producing an impeccable manuscript and to Alison Graham for her skilled copy-editing.

For the medical staff in Barnstaple, the Kent and Sussex Hospital in Tunbridge Wells, the Harley Street Clinic; for my caring GP in Crowborough and the paramedics in Devon and Sussex; for the practical love of the staff and members of All Saints Church, Crowborough; for the support of *Renewal*'s staff especially in 1993; and for Ann who encouraged me to write this book while knowing how painful she would find it to read; for everyone of them I give thanks to God.

Foreword

It is a sombre fact of life that the lessons we learn hardest are often those we learn best. But it need not always be so. Sometimes it is possible, that if others are honest with us, we can learn from their experiences. As I read this book I felt as if I was peering over Edward England's shoulder and at times actually feeling the experiences he was going through.

Edward has had a long and fruitful life and there are millions of people all around the world who thank God for the books he has brought to them as a publisher. Of course he has often been behind the scenes in that; few people realise that were it not for his foresight many of us would never have read titles like *Ordering Your Private World* by Gordon MacDonald. All that is true, nevertheless I have a hunch that in years to come countless people will thank him for bringing to us *his* story in *The Addiction of a Busy Life*.

The addiction that Edward speaks of is a killer indeed. I have seen it destroy churches, marriages and rob gifted people of the ability to perform. There are children who have missed out on a father or mother because of this scourge and yet for all its potency we allow it, even encourage it, to grow silently in our lives.

There are dramatic moments in this book. The heart attack hits Edward as he is alone on a hilltop walk and you may well sense, as I did, the sheer terror of his hasting to get help and yet every step producing excruciating pain. But it is on that hilltop that the lessons begin that will change his life for ever and eventually give us this book. Take time not only to read but to ponder its message. Read a passage and then walk a little and let it seep into your spirit. A million things will conspire to stop you doing that – all of them worthwhile and most of them screaming urgency. But the great urgency is that you and I have time to think about our lives – the people we love and the God we serve and the things that are of most importance.

In this book Edward England has given us a gift, he has given us himself. The incredible result of that is that if we are wise and God helps us, we can learn the lessons that he has experienced through great trauma but a little more easily. For him they were forged out of pain on a lonely South Downs path. You and I don't have to walk that path – just take time to read of it and ask God's help that as we read we are changed . . . and liberated.

Rob Parsons
Executive Director,
Care for the Family

Chapter One

What time is it in your life? Imagine your life as a clock without hands, and you have to draw in the hands. Where would you put them?

Ann asked the question as we were walking on a cloudless day on the South Downs Way. It wasn't an original question but it was new to me. She had found it in *Life Path*, a book on journal writing which the author, Luci Shaw, had left with us after she stayed in our home. Ann was into journal writing. Luci's husband, Harold, had been my favourite American publisher. He had died of cancer.

'If,' Ann repeated, 'you were putting in the hands on your clock, where would you place them?'

'You're asking how long do I think I have to live,' I murmured. It was not a typical question from my wife: usually hers were more likely to be about what would I like for lunch, where should we go for our holidays, did she need to visit the hairdressers, or if she was really stuck on *The Times* crossword something like what is a fabric wrap in five letters? Before I had grasped the clue she would be writing shawl, or whatever. *What time is it in your life?* was rather more serious.

I was in my early sixties, reasonably fit, and had not

been in a hospital ward since I was nine, except as a visitor. I didn't even know the name of my doctor, one of several in the surgery where I was registered. My father, grandfather and great grandfather had lived into their seventies, most days spending long hours in the garden. With present-day medical care I might last longer, perhaps into my eighties.Who knows? So I was taken aback by my own answer, unsure where it came from.

'I think it's probably five to twelve.'

Ann didn't reply, her eyes on the newborn lambs in the adjoining field. Is there a more delightful sight? They watched our approach warily then, led by the ewes, retreated as we drew close. They had no concept of the brevity of life and I would have probably forgotten our hilltop conversation but for what happened later.

I was in the early stages of walking the South Downs Way in Sussex, with Ann joining me on some days, to tone up my muscles, because everyone said exercise was good, and for the sheer enjoyment and beauty of the views. The Way stretches some ninety-nine miles from Eastbourne to Winchester, across the finest country in south-east England: a magnet for walkers and artists. The starting point has the immense advantage of being only thirty miles from home. I planned on my day off each week to walk nine or ten miles. Only on fine and sunny days: not too cold, not too hot. I would hardly make the *Guinness Book of Records*. A serious walker would have regarded my distance as an afternoon stroll. A seventy-year-old, Henry Bridge, had apparently walked the entire length of the Way in thirty-four hours. Most people took a week to ten days. I reckoned on three months.

The Way is linked to a track originating 2,000 years before the Romans came. The chalk uplands were known to Stone Age people as a safe path, away from the dangerous forests below. A number of burial sites have been identified.

Ann was not with me on a glorious May Sunday when I set out on the eight-and-a-half-mile stretch, which would take me to one of the highest points on the Downs, Chanctonbury Ring, forty or so miles from Eastbourne. The ring of trees visible from thirty miles away marks an Iron Age hill-fort. It can be a windy place but as I set out from Upper Beeding there was barely a breath of breeze. The sun was shining. Ann had nobly stayed at home to pack our cases for our visit to Lee Abbey in Devon, where from Monday I was leading a six-day writers' conference. She waved me off with a wistful look and a prayer: 'Bless him, Lord.'

I was to need that prayer.

I decided to celebrate each step of the walk. After crossing the bridge over the Adur I took a few minutes to visit the thirteenth-century church of St Botolph's, but could see only the exterior as the doors were locked. A fear of vandalism?

A steady ninety-minute climb followed. The South Downs Way signposts were thoughtfully situated so that my map was barely needed. When I paused for a break I treated myself to a square of chocolate or an apple. My pauses lasted three or four minutes. Most walkers would not have taken them. There was no shelter from the sun and I put on the white summer hat I had bought in Zermatt the previous year. High on the Downs I crossed a country road, watched the hang-gliding, and saw the sea in the distance at Worthing.

A few hundred yards before reaching Chanctonbury Ring and the shadow of the beech trees I passed a BBC television van. I guessed the camera crew were somewhere making a documentary. Near the trees I sank down on the grass, relishing the distant view of the

Weald. I imagined I could see our house in Crowborough Warren, twenty-five miles away. I could certainly see where Crowborough was.

I unbuckled my pack and took out the tasty ham sandwiches which Ann had made. The lunch pack was a highlight of any walk. As I munched, a police helicopter buzzed briefly overhead, patrolling the Downs. I had almost finished my sandwiches by the time it disappeared, a tiny dot in the distance.

Chanctonbury Ring is a favourite spot for families to congregate as it is accessible by road. I could hear children's voices as I stretched out contentedly on the grass, the almost empty haversack under my head. I closed my eyes, wondering what Ann was doing, feeling the warmth of the sun on my face, thankful my Lee Abbey talks were prepared. Delivering them was the easy part.

I had stood at that lecture rostrum many times in the last thirteen years, at conferences lasting five to seven days. These retreats from normal life were associated with the happiest memories. At first the wardens had been John and Gay Perry. John was now a bishop, and his place had been taken by Mike Edson.

Although the ground was hard, the longer I rested the less inclined I was to get up and start walking. Eventually I dragged myself to my feet, put the rucksack on my back and slowly made towards the gate by the dew-pond. The rest of the walk was downhill and, being the hottest time of the day, I was glad. The path dropped some 750 feet to the tiny village of Washington.

After a few steps my pack became unbelievably heavy, as if someone had filled it with rocks. I had barely noticed it on my back when it contained the sandwiches and coffee: why should it be so irksome now? I hitched it from my back to carry it in my left hand, then transferred it to the right. A fearsome pain in my arms and the back of my shoulders intensified. Whichever way I held the virtually empty rucksack it weighed a ton. I'd proceed slowly, and rest frequently until the pain eased.

I scarcely moved. Washington, with its church, pub and scattered houses was in the distance, at the foot of a long, winding gravelled track. I picked out the church tower.

'Dear God, what's wrong? I walked up that hill without difficulty, why this problem when I'm going down? Help me.'

The pain intensified and I sweated heavily as it spread from my back and arms across my chest. A heavy unrelenting weight.

The BBC van was now well behind. If I went back for help I'd have to climb again. It's probably the sensible thing to do, I thought, but continued on.

Heart attack? I swallowed hard and tried to dismiss the possibility. I had never seen anyone have one. Did they start like this? I recalled reading Catherine Marshall's *Peter Marshall*, in which she told how Peter, a minister in his forties, had experienced a heart attack in the night, and was rushed to hospital. He died before breakfast. Had Peter hurt like this? I had never talked with Catherine about it.

Strangely, I was unconcerned about the long-term effect of a heart attack, but only whether it would prevent my going to Lee Abbey. The engagement had been in my diary almost a year. I couldn't, wouldn't let them down. Only once, because of heavy snow, had I cancelled an engagement. A less important one. It was a matter of honour, reputation to be there.

I could have thrown the cheap rucksack away and don't know why I didn't, although it weighed hardly anything. I looked wistfully for the helicopter as I sat on the bank alongside the track for a longer rest. I needed help. An ambulance couldn't get up this track but a helicopter would find a way of reaching me. I'd wave my arms to attract attention.

'Don't dramatise the situation,' the rational side of my mind urged. 'You're never ill.'

'I can't take any more of this pain,' my body cried.

The stops grew longer as with head down and bowed shoulders I was forced to rest every few yards on the grassy bank. 'Think positively,' I told myself. 'It's possible to break through the pain barrier.'

Had I eaten the sandwiches too quickly, got sunstroke, or just over-stretched myself? I should have sought the shelter of the trees, or waited for lunch until the day's walk was completed.

'God, would you have allowed me to accept the Lee Abbey invitation if you'd not intended me to go? I must be there. Please take away this trouble.'

I heard conversation and footsteps behind. A sun-tanned couple, in their twenties, in walking attire. I sank down on the verge and watched them approach. They'd offer me an arm, a shoulder, assist me to the main road if I asked them. But I was too proud. They strode past, chattering, with barely a glance.

Months afterwards the thought came that this couple might have been the answer to my prayer, if not the one I sought. I did not want to be embarrassed. So I just went on, a few yards, a rest, further steps, another pause. The pain would pass. Everything does. After all I was going downhill.

'Ann, I need you now,' I exclaimed aloud. Being a doctor she'd know what to do, take charge; no outward panic, whatever was going on inside. As sweat ran down my forehead and cheeks I removed my glasses and reached for a handkerchief.

Did heart trouble run in families? There was my

father's stroke, his brother's heart failure in the night. Ann would know. I'd stopped thinking positively. You have to be fit to do that.

The main road to Worthing, skirting the village, was becoming clearer. Dinky-sized cars. If I could reach there I'd flag down the first car; if it didn't stop I'd stand in the middle of the road and compel the next, seeking a lift to Worthing. With all those retired people there must be a hospital. Speedier than waiting for an ambulance.

If I could make the road.

It took a long time but I did. There was a stile at the point where the Downs Way reached the road. I sat on the step half-seeing cars go by, standing to let a bulky man clamber over while his dog squeezed through a gap in the hedge. A house opposite, someone hanging out washing. If I asked they might let me use a phone and rest until an ambulance arrived. Even if they kept me in over night, Ann could take me home tomorrow, and I'd still make it to Lee Abbey.

A new thought. Was there a public phone-box in the village? A short walk. I crawled along the pavement and stumbled to Washington's historic Street to look for a red kiosk. There wasn't one. Nobody around. I pushed the door of the ancient parish church. There was no one there. Sinking in a pew I remained for an hour undisturbed, bowed but not entirely in prayer. A good place to die, I thought. A friend had died in church – in the middle of preaching a Sunday evening sermon. I needed a drink but could not find a tap in the church, although I reasoned there must be one somewhere for the font and the flowers. I searched desperately.

I remembered a story I'd read years ago. A hyperactive, middle-aged businessman, sales director type, racing home in his big car after an arduous day, foot hard down, anxious to reach his wife and children, ignoring the speed limit. An overpowering chest pain. Panic. He pulls into the kerb, opens the windows, gulps in fresh air. Eventually, he compels himself to drive on, slowly now, to find a phone-box. As he dials he sinks to the floor unconscious.

I was more fortunate. After sixty minutes in the church the pain gradually began to subside. I could stand up straight, lift my arms, hold my pack.

'Thank you, Lord, I'm not going to die. An awful shock if I did for the worshippers on Sunday morning.'

Unsteady on my feet, I stepped into the bright daylight. Along the Street there was a left turn, a short winding road, a downward slope with a few modern houses, leading to the village inn. The Franklin Arms had been a stopping place for walkers since 1820. I shuffled along. Families sat in the sun at the wooden tables loaded with glasses, lingering over the remains of lunch, their children playing on the lawn.

I ordered the largest glass of orange juice and sat brooding over it for another hour, knowing I might have died on that hillside or in the church. How inconvenient, how thoughtless that would have been. The drink was refreshing. I wondered whether to order another, but feeling better walked charily to the bar. Forget hospital, I'd get back to my car. Perhaps it was all the consequence of exhaustion, a sedentary life.

'Can I get a taxi?' I asked the barman.

After one orange juice? He looked surprised. He pointed to the pay phone at the end of the counter. 'You'll find the number there.'

'About ten minutes, sir,' a girl's voice promised.

I sat on the low wall outside, impatiently waiting, thankful the pain had gone.

'Lee Abbey, here I come!'

In retrospect I ask what made me think I could ignore

the warning I'd been given? What idiocy, what image of self-importance drove me on? God normally speaks to us in whispers; in this case there had been a shout. Perhaps I had got away with too much in my life before.

It was right of course to have a sense of responsibility for the conference, for the hundred or so authors and potential authors attending. The other two speakers, both established writers, had not been there before. In my thinking, retreat from commitment was unforgivable. Or was pride the problem? Reputation? A fear of exposing any weakness, however obvious it might already be?

I should have known better. God could manage without me; Lee Abbey would survive; the other speakers would rise to the challenge. He can always afford to give his workers a break. But I was not in a mood for listening. My diary said Lee Abbey and I intended to be there. On Monday. On time. No delaying to visit the surgery. The break from office life, the change of location, the bracing sea air, the rural scenes, the spacious house, the seashore, the like-minded people, all had been keenly anticipated. How could they manage without me?

Over the coming months I would have to learn many lessons; struggling with some, happily accepting others. Like most adults I was not looking for personal change. It was easier to go 'with the flow'. I appreciated life the way I lived it. So it meant I was totally unprepared to respond to the first lesson I was being taught that May Saturday, not in a lecture hall or a church, but on the Downs. If my ears had been unblocked, my heart receptive, I would have prevented much pain for Ann and myself. As a needed reminder to me and to others, I record what has become so clear in retrospect:

God speaks to us through our bodies.

GOD SPEAKS TO US THROUGH OUR BODIES

The protests of the body are the alarm signals.
—Dr Paul Tournier

The great Christians knew well that man has a body too.
The greatest of them knew how important that body was.
—Dr William Barclay

In hospital I began to consider that in trying to do all those worthy things that everybody wanted me to do, I had become the subject of a tyrannical schedule rather than God's priorities.

—Charles Colson

. . . has been laid on a bed of sickness and is agonising about duties not performed. Is it possible, Lord, that upon occasion you must 'make' us to lie down in green pastures to get our attention?

Enable us to see each temporarily closed door as your leading towards the green pastures and the still waters of a listening ear and a receptive and obedient heart.
—Catherine Marshall

Chapter Two

The word 'addict' brings to mind pictures of dope-fiends, empty eyes, dirty syringes, derelict buildings, prostitution and petty crime. We've seen them portrayed so often in television documentaries or met them in real life. But there are other types of addicts: well-scrubbed people, living in tree-lined roads, with regular incomes, wearing smart clothes, worshipping regularly in church. Sometimes they occupy the pulpit, live in the vicarage, lead Christian organisations or hold high positions in the church hierarchy.

The truth broke on me during a winter holiday three months before my planned visit to Lee Abbey.

We had needed a break from February's drizzle and mist, the gloomy days, the dripping, swaying trees which surrounded our home. We collected a variety of brochures, with colourful images of beaches, palm trees, cloudless skies: and chose Madeira. Lush semi-tropical vegetation, stunning mountain scenery and near perfect climate, within four hours flight, we read and believed. We were thirty-five minutes from Gatwick airport. We'd buy a week of sunshine.

'Let's go,' I said, with the urgency I expressed about everything. Ann doesn't have the haste-disease and likes to plan carefully. 'You can find a locum for your clinics.'

She responded with the inevitable questions. 'What shall I wear?' I was wise enough not to answer. 'Are you sure it'll be sunny?'

The brochure says, 'Sunny skies, and a temperature well above ours.'

We savoured the mountain peaks, banana plantations, fishermen's coves and complained about the mediocre weather. No one in the pool. Raincoats were carried most days. Our hotel in Machico, with stony beach, wide bay and fifteenth-century church, provided us with a small bedroom, compensated for by three spacious lounges, ideal for page-turning books and long hours together.

On holiday Ann enjoyed the classics and detective stories. I took Keath Fraser's *Worst Journeys*, a Picador paperback, in which doughty travellers told of experiences of tribulation or near disaster, often in blistering heat or crippling cold. It was snug to participate in their misfortune in the comfort and security of an armchair, a handsome dark-haired waiter with tea-trolley within call. As Paul Theroux drily observed: 'The worst journeys often made the best reading.'

Most contributions to *Worst Journeys* were so compelling that I knew I would turn to them a second time. One was quite different. David Mamet described a family holiday he was reluctant to take. When he finally arrived in the Caribbean he kept saying to himself: 'I am here, I'm spending good money, everything is wrong. . . . Make it different or I'm going home.'

Mamet had arrived on holiday exhausted as I had. He slept for eighteen hours on each of the first two days, then on the third day the holiday got going for him and he had a glorious time, having leisurely breakfasts on the patio, swimming and water skiing.

He realised something was happening to him; he was having a break from *the addiction of a busy life*. As I read those words I confronted and acknowledged the truth about myself. A moment of honesty followed:

'Lord, I am an addict of a busy life. I have been for twenty-five years, ever since I joined Hodder and Stoughton and now more than ever, running my own enterprise. I don't think I can help it. It's the way I'm made.'

I relished being busy, initiating projects, being immersed in books and magazines, and numerous church activities. I was drawn by working communities rather than worshipping ones. By choice, I attended a busy church.

Yet the diagnosis came as a shock. To be addicted sounded less appealing than to be committed. To be committed was praiseworthy – but to be addicted? How had it happened? What could I do? No point in asking my clergy friends. Those I appreciated most, my shining examples, were addicts too.

I glanced at Ann. We'd been married fifteen years. My first wife, Gwen, had died of lung cancer: no, she'd never smoked. Now it seemed I'd spent all my life with Ann. Happy years. And Gwen would have approved. That mattered to me. Ann had been on her daily prayer list for years while Ann served as a missionary in a remote Thai hospital.

She was now absorbed in her painting, watercolours, as we sat facing out over the bay.

'Ann, do you know I'm an addict?' I asked, breaking her concentration. 'An addict of a busy life?'

'I haven't got those clouds quite right,' she said non-chalantly, but listened carefully as I insisted on telling her about David Mamet, reading the key passage. Good books had always fired me.

'You had to come to Madeira to find that out?' she asked, as a lone seagull soared across the wide windows, her attention already refocused.

I must apply the brakes, perhaps start painting, taking time to look, to stare at the world around; to see, as Ann saw, the petals of a flower, the shape of a rock, the nest in a tree, the light and shade of the land and sea, the silhouette of trees. She had been on a tree painting weekend. 'Nothing but trees?' I asked unbelievingly, on her return.

My addiction was rooted in an inner restlessness that had marked my life. A new challenge always beckoned. I hoped it had a beneficial as well as a negative aspect.

'But now I'm fatigued and living in a world of burned-out people,' I reflected. 'The pressure is taking its toll.'

Twenty years ago, Paul Hodder-Williams, chairman of Hodder and Stoughton, had written of my amazing capacity for work. I liked it. Among talented colleagues, who'd made their way academically, there was little else notable about me, but in the last twelve months I had known the consequences: exhaustion, disturbed nights, lapses in concentration, and I was leaning more heavily on my staff. They had been God's special gift to me.

My Yorkshire family had believed in hard work, long hours on five, often six days a week, with Sundays reserved for church. I had started my career as a trainee journalist with a Sheffield daily newspaper, reporting coroners' courts, colliery and road accidents, golden weddings, local church activities, usually centred around the Cathedral or the thriving Methodist churches, which in those days attracted large congregations.

Good-humoured, tolerant, older journalists had encouraged me to do some feature writing, and I would happily take home the newspaper with my name alongside the article. My father was uninterested. For him, in those days, there was one newspaper, *The Manchester Guardian*.

I had a few press photos from those days. In one taken in 1947, when Europe had its worst winter, I was surrounded by snow drifts six feet high, as with a photographer I tried to get from Sheffield to a Derbyshire village which had been cut off for weeks. We didn't make it but a stream train engine eventually made it through to bring out a pregnant woman in urgent need of hospital attention. I wrote stories of newborn babies in houses without fuel or any heating, of temperatures that lingered below freezing for almost two months.

Journalism led to children's books, the first about a junior reporter; and then along a twisting road in my mid-thirties to an appointment as an editor, and later a director, of the old-established London publisher, Hodder and Stoughton. My office windows were no longer covered with soot from industrial chimneys: from one I overlooked St Paul's Cathedral, from another the scales of justice on the Old Bailey. I could scarcely believe my good fortune.

Hodders, founded almost a century earlier, was a happy company as well as a prestigious one. Top novelists like John LeCarre, Elizabeth Goudge and Mary Stewart, senior politicians, archbishops, cardinals, and international figures like Dr Martin Luther King, were part of our world. We visited them in their homes, they dined in our offices. Good books, not profit, was our motivation.

For a period I looked after the firm's publicity, as well as its religious books, and a handful of general authors. But my heart was set on developing the religious list, restoring it to the glory of early years.

I had never seen so many intently active people as there were in this company. My predecessor, Leonard

Cutts, reached the office before 8 am after an hour's journey from Kent. Until my arrival, in addition to religious books he edited the famous *Teach Yourself* series, 600 titles, sitting up in bed many nights with a manuscript.

Earlier in the century, another famous Hodder editor, William Robertson Nicoll, baffled his colleagues with his output. His biographer described him as being three men at once: a powerful editor, a writer of tireless industry, and a stalwart politician. A lady novelist once asked him what kinds of books the public were looking for. 'I don't know – except this – that they will always want *good* books. If you do a good book of whatever kind, you need not fear,' he replied.

In one of his last letters from his home in Hampstead he wrote: 'Being exceedingly worn out, I gave in my resignation at Hodder and Stoughton. I felt I could not be responsible even for the reduced amount of work I do. I feel I must have a few months leave of absolute quietness and no work at all.'

He can be forgiven for his tiredness. He was seventy.

In conferences and writers' seminars in America, South Africa, Singapore, Australia and New Zealand, I had taught that Hodders looked for authors who would work at it. I had told of John Creasey, a crime writer, whose books I had been responsible for during one two-year stretch. Creasey wrote 536 novels before his premature death. Sitting in his mansion near Salisbury he pointed out with pride the hundreds of translations which surrounded him on the book-lined walls. Impressive for a former cabinet-maker who had once been unemployed.

'I can write a book in three weeks,' he boasted. It was true.

Thackeray was another author I admired. 'As soon as

one piece of work is out of hand,' he wrote, 'and before going to sleep, I like to begin another; it may be to write only half a dozen lines.'

My favourite religious author was Canon David Watson, Anglican clergyman and evangelist. David was warned by his doctor of his self-destructive schedule of activity. Even after major surgery for cancer he continued speaking at lunches, dinners, church services and festivals; making a memorable BBC broadcast, 'A case for healing', which prompted hundreds of letters.

God spoke to him in the early hours of one morning. 'He showed me,' David wrote, 'that all my preaching, writing and other ministry was absolutely nothing compared to my love relationship with him. In fact my sheer busyness had squeezed out the intimacy I had known with him during the first few months after my operation.' He went on, 'Whatever else is happening to me physically, God is working deeply in my life. His challenge to me can be summed up in three words, "Seek my face".'

He died in February 1984. He was fifty. Only in death did he find release from his addiction. At a service of thanksgiving in York Minster, Stuart Blanch, Archbishop of York, said, 'He was a shining and a burning light, but shining and burning is a costly business and it took its toll.'

I left Hodder in 1980 and launched a literary agency. Soon I had more than 100 authors on my books. I took over *Renewal* magazine, first as publisher then as both publisher and editor, launched *Healing and Wholeness*, and Highland Books, and was planning a third magazine. In my free time, I served on the board of several organisations, including Renovare, founded by Dr Richard Foster. Its aim was to develop a balanced vision of Christian life and faith and a practical strategy for personal spiritual growth – and much more. The previous year I had been to join Richard and others in speaking at a Renovare conference in Wichita. There we all learned about the five major disciplines found in the life of Christ and the corresponding five streams of life in Christian faith and witness: what some call the contemplative, the holiness, the charismatic, the social justice, and the evangelical traditions. It was one of those glorious weekends which Richard would describe as high, holy and hilarious.

On the way back I stopped for two nights in New York to see Gordon MacDonald, author of *Ordering Your Private World* which had been awarded the gold medallion for the best devotional book of the year. Over a simple meal, in a restaurant situated between his home and the church where he was pastor, he spoke of how New York was full of abnormally busy people, usually too busy for ordinary relationships. He had found breakfast at 6.30 am in a local cafe the best time to meet some of his congregation – there was no other space in their schedule.

He mentioned pastors who were also driven. Some had been known to burn out scores of assistants and lay leaders because of their need to head organisations that were the biggest, the best and the most well known. In his bestselling book he had written of how Paul the apostle in his pre-Christian days was driven.

As a driven man, he studied, he joined, he attained, he defended and he was applauded. The pace at which he was operating shortly before his conversion was almost manic. He was driven towards some illusive goal, and, later, when he could look back at that lifestyle with all of its compulsions, he would say, 'It was all worthless.'

Paul was driven until Christ called him. He was changed from a driven man into a called one on the

Damascus road when, in complete submission, he asked Jesus Christ, 'What shall I do, Lord?'

But some of us had started off called and finished up driven. Could we be changed?

Most certainly. It begins when such a person faces up to the fact that he is operating according to drives and not calls. . . . To deal with drivenness, one must begin ruthlessly to appraise his motives and values just as Peter was forced to do in his periodic confrontations with Jesus.

To spend time with men like Richard Foster and Gordon MacDonald was stimulating and humbling. Flying home I knew I was privileged. Strange then, that for a month afterwards, I was running on empty. Somewhere my life was out of balance.

For a couple of years I had been a warden of All Saints Church, Crowborough, in East Sussex, where Andrew Cornes, with two other clergy, ministered to a crowded and appreciative church. There are few finer parish churches: not the Victorian building but the gifted clergy and warm-hearted people, the twenty or so housegroups meeting on a fortnightly basis for Bible study. We belonged to a fine one led by Peter and Rosemary Scott. Young couples move to Crowborough to become members of All Saints.

We were contemplating a £2.3 million extension. Many evenings we received a phone call at home expressing strong views for or against. The vicar asked me if I would give the sermon on the Sunday morning before one crucial vote. I preached on the words of Jesus in Luke 14:25–35 – 'For which of you, desiring to build a tower, does not first sit down and count the cost, whether he has enough to complete it?' It was folly, Jesus suggested, to build and not first to count the cost. He underlined this in verses 31 and 32: 'No man should go

27

to war, without considering the hazard of it.' In modern parlance, look before you leap.

Jesus was not saying this man should not build the tower. In fact, he was implying that he should, but only when he had counted the cost.

I'm convinced of the benefit of the extension. I'm grateful to our building committee and the architects for their magnificent vision, and I'm a little scared, and I hope you are too. By going ahead we'll be making a major contribution to the gospel in this town for the next 100 years, but is it too heavy a burden for us to bear? There is no surplus money in many homes. Parents are sacrificing for their children, or looking after elderly relatives, or struggling with a mortgage. And some are worried about their jobs.

I believe we only have a right to vote yes if we are willing with God's help to give sacrificially. For some that may be the widow's mite, for others a few hundred pounds over five years, for some thousands. It is so easy to vote yes for any imaginative proposal but saying yes on this occasion implies a willingness to give until it hurts.

I'll be sad if we say no to some form of major extension because this is the great opportunity to put our faith into practice, to move into a new dimension in our walk with God, to realise that ours is a God of the impossible.

Another year or so passed before the congregation, with a sufficiently overwhelming majority, voted to proceed with the full development. The period for reflection was necessary. There had to be a time for counting the cost. I had not sought re-election as a warden but when the vote was counted I was proud to belong to All Saints. The church and the preaching suited my temperament. There was none in the diocese more active, whose members were more involved. Henry Ward Beecher would have found acceptance in our pulpit when he said, 'Blessed be the man whose work drives him. Something must drive men; and if it is wholesome industry, they may not have time for a thousand torments and temptations.'

All Saints, like most evangelical communities, had few contemplatives among the 600 or 700 who worshipped there. We were hardly likely to quote Mother Teresa's words: 'By contemplation the soul draws directly from the heart of God the graces which the active life must distribute.'

For me it all added up to a fulfilling life of action, but I was to discover that God did not consider Edward England as important as my interests might imply, and as my *Filofax* led me to think. He was astonishingly unimpressed. My services voluntary and otherwise could be dispensed with altogether.

I was far from the point where I wanted to heed the advice of that prince of preachers, Dr Charles H. Spurgeon, but his words would eventually become my second lesson:

Learning to stop is the first step on the road back to sanity.

The Second Lesson

LEARNING TO STOP IS THE FIRST STEP ON THE ROAD BACK TO SANITY

Be still before the Lord, and wait patiently for him.
—Psalm 37:7 (RSV)

Stop and consider God's wonders.
—Job 37:14 (NIV)

Rest. Rest. Rest in God's love. The only work you are required now to do is to give your most intense attention to his still, small voice within.

—Madame Jeanne Guyon

You can be tired in the work and not tired of the work. It is possible that a man has been over-working – I do not care in what realm, whether natural or spiritual – and over-taxing his energy and his physical resources. If you go on working too hard or under strain you are bound to suffer. And of course if that is the trouble, the remedy you need is medical treatment.

There is a striking example in the Old Testament. You remember that when Elijah had that attack of spiritual depression after his historic effort on Mt Carmel, he sat down under a juniper tree and felt sorry for himself. But the real thing he needed was sleep and food; and God gave him both. He gave some food and rest before he gave him spiritual help.

—Dr Martyn Lloyd-Jones, Spiritual Depression

What is the point of so much of our busyness and of our hurry and our worry and our effort and our anxiety?

We strive so hard to get a little farther up the ladder – but in the end, what's the point of it all? What good is it really going to do us? Even if the things we worry about do happen, the heavens won't collapse.

—Dr William Barclay

Chapter Three

'It wasn't a heart attack,' I told myself firmly as I stepped with relief from the taxi at the small parking place by the roundabout where I'd left my car that morning. The taxi-driver, a woman I guess in her seventies, had raced along the narrow country roads at a terrifying speed, her patter keeping up with the mileage.

With thankfulness I opened the door of my own car and sank into the seat, gazing up at the green, ever-changing Downs. Hopefully in a few weeks I'd complete the journey by foot to Winchester – it had become a city of dreams – but I'd pace myself, avoid the mid-day sun, have a meal at the end rather than during the walk.

I was a trifle scared. A few hours earlier I hadn't thought I'd make it to the road, seeing myself on a stretcher, despatched to hospital. But I had made it without assistance. If my condition had been serious I wouldn't have recovered with a couple of hours' rest. It would have taken days, weeks.

Absolutely nothing to worry about. Weren't all men hypochondriacs?

I drove the car home slowly, being overtaken rather than overtaking as was usual, pondering what, if anything, I should say to Ann. I pulled in once and drained a small carton of orange juice. We kept several in the car in case we were caught in a jam in sweltering heat on the motorway.

Ann wouldn't panic if I told her. She'd been involved in too many serious emergency situations in the mission hospital, surrounded by paddy fields in Thailand. Patients, often accompanied by numerous family members, with gun-shot wounds, head injuries, mangled limbs, and expectant mothers with complications, arrived seeking skilled treatment. In her second term, as an obstetrician, the obstetrics and gynaecology unit had been her special concern.

I'd underplay it a bit, not risk jeopardising our presence at the writers' conference. I drove steadily through Haywards Heath, along the road which crossed the Ashdown Forest, past a warning roadside sign to beware of deer. I'd never seen one around here but Ann had.

'Had a good day?' she asked breezily as I turned the latch key, opened the front door, and saw her at the end of the hall, with an almost packed suitcase on the floor, neatly folded shirts in tissue. 'I felt envious when your car pulled into the road. I know it was my choice to stay behind.'

A quick hug. It was heartening to be home with her, secure in a world of easy chairs, a waiting bed, a telephone. Ann had obviously concentrated on the packing – travel had taught her how to squeeze a wardrobe into a suitcase. She insisted on doing it, working from lists, missing nothing. Who was I to complain?

'You enjoyed the Downs? They must have been at their best.'

'Yes, terrific. Mind it was a bit of a pull today, rather warm, with no shelter on the ridge. Magnificent views. I think I could see Crowborough. After lunch . . .' I paused.

'Something wrong with the sandwiches?'

'Delicious. It was afterwards, when I picked up the rucksack, almost empty. It seemed as if it was full of stones. Pains in my arms, my back. I'd finished climbing, so it was downhill then. Had a long rest at the bottom. That's what I needed.'

'How long did the pain last?' I could see her anxious look. 'I'll make you some tea.' I followed her into the kitchen as she put a teabag in the pot.

'It was most of all in my back, behind the shoulders. I'm better now. The pain, completely gone. I phoned for a taxi back to the car. A scary woman driver. A bit extravagant but I didn't want to hang around for country buses.'

'Were you frightened?'

'A bit.' I hesitated. 'I don't think I've ever felt so ill.'

'Should I call Dr Sampson?' I'd apparently met him at a party for doctors and nurses and was registered with him.

'We'll phone him if the pain returns,' I promised. 'What I really need is a nap on the bed. Just for an hour.'

'Call me if you need me,' Ann instructed as she gave me a mug of tea and drew the curtains. 'I'll leave the bedroom door open a little so I can hear you.'

She returned to her preparations for departure. She always left the house spotless, every magazine, towel, chair in place. Eric, our next-door neighbour, kept an eye on it during our absence, watering plants, stacking mail on the desk, once getting up in the early hours to investigate when the burglar alarm went off. A faulty part.

I immediately fell asleep. Two hours later a hot bath, which should have relaxed me, instead left me breathless. Unusually so. I did not linger in the steam-filled atmosphere. Over supper I made confident, reassuring noises and the next morning, energy restored, we attended the service at All Saints. I was fit again, yesterday's warning forgotten.

We had planned to drive to Lee Abbey, some 230 miles, on Monday, arriving in time for me to address the opening evening session. This session always set the tone for the whole conference so I had given careful thought to what to say.

'I think,' Ann proposed after Sunday lunch, 'as we're already packed, it might be good to drive down the M4 to Bristol today and stay overnight in the motorway lodge as we did the year we went to Cornwall.' We had appreciated the convenience of the snug bedroom, the colour television and teasmade.

'Then we could call and see Wells Cathedral in the morning, and drive leisurely across Exmoor in the afternoon,' I agreed. 'Be at Lee Abbey in time for tea.'

Lee Abbey is a lay community of some seventy people of all ages, nationalities and denominations. The common denominator is faith in Christ. The community, while it cares for an estate of 260 acres, welcomes guests to share with them the blessings they have received.

Wells Cathedral fired our imagination. It was years since we had last visited. As we quietly moved within its great stone walls we were aware of the worship of Christians on this site for more than 1,000 years. There was an attractive leaflet with a message from the Dean, Richard Lewis:

> You stand in a holy place where, day by day, God is worshipped, sometimes with spoken words, sometimes in silence, sometimes with glorious music from the organ, and from our choir. Walk around this Cathedral Church. Marvel at its beauty. Think of the faith which built it and sustains it still. It tells its own story as you talk quietly, walk softly and think deeply.

It was a hallowed hour for us at the start of a busy week, talking quietly, walking softly, if not thinking deeply.

'I wish we could call in for a coffee with George Carey,' I said.

Dr Carey had been Bishop of Bath and Wells before becoming Archbishop of Canterbury. I had been his publisher in the 1970s and his literary agent for thirteen years. We recalled the day when it was announced he was going to Canterbury. A few weeks before I had been negotiating a book contract for him.

'If you become the next Archbishop of Canterbury,' I wrote, 'I could secure a more worthy advance!' He had only recently gone to Bath and Wells. It was premature to think of him at Lambeth.

When Ann telephoned me at the office to tell me his appointment as Archbishop had been announced on the mid-day news, I didn't believe her.

'You're joking,' I insisted. 'Maybe next time round.'

'I'm not. It is the number one news item. It's true, it's true,' she maintained gladly.

'That's unbelievably wonderful,' I exclaimed.

For more than twenty years I had been making visits to Lambeth Palace to meet the Archbishops for whom Hodder published: Fisher, Coggan, Ramsey and for a biography by Margaret Duggan of Runcie. Now it would be to see Archbishop Carey. I had observed at close range the pressures on the Primate, seen how each coped. I was sure George Carey would sometimes wish he were back in this quieter place.

He probably knew the story about Alexander the Great, who around 334 BC, when he had conquered the Persian Empire and marched his army into Northern India, found himself facing a rebellion by his most loyal men. He asked his officers for an explanation. One dared to tell him: 'Sir, if there is one thing above all others a successful man like you should know – it is when to stop.'

That would be the biggest challenge George Carey would have to face. Knowing when to stop, when to rest, relax, be recharged. He had never been a part of the leisured classes. Even before Canterbury he had started work at 6.30 am – writing books, preparing sermons. Publishers were invariably chasing him for another title.

As many as 25% of all clergy are addicts of the busy life syndrome. Among evangelicals the percentage is undoubtedly higher. At parish level they struggle to be 110% vicars. The more gifted among them, in addition to parish responsibilities, are often rural deans, chairmen of ecclesiastical gatherings, preachers at conventions, mission leaders. 'Better to burn out for Christ than rust out.' While they urge their congregations to spend more time in prayer they often live life at too fast a pace to provide an example.

As we pulled into the grounds of Lee Abbey we looked for the sheep. Every spring about 150 ewes produce mostly twins, with a smattering of triplets and singles. It was part of our holiday to watch them, the sea in the background

'I hope they give us the usual room,' Ann said. The double bedroom, overlooking the sea, adjacent to the library and the chaplain's suite, had normally been our base.

I was temporarily downhearted when we were shown to another room. Ann was devastated. She wrote in her journal:

It was so disappointing not to be in the room we are usually in, known, familiar, a spiritual place where we've talked with people, which has been our home for previous visits. It is awful to feel so upset – we have a perfectly good room –

in a way more room to move around but it's not the same.

We have a sea view but it's marred by a tree. One of the joys of coming back was to a known place, loved and appreciated. I could have cried when we arrived, and did not want to unpack. I've never felt like this at Lee Abbey before. I don't cope with disappointment very well – please help me to learn from you about this, Lord. The sea, the cove, the cliffs are as beautiful as ever – you are here. Please help me, please help Edward.

Over supper we talked with the two other speakers, Marion Stroud, whose books had been translated into a total of fourteen languages, and Merrilyn Williams, once Paul Gallico's secretary, who was going to share her expertise on writing biography and autobiography.

I gave my first talk to about eighty guests, including experienced writers and beginners, who were seeking ideas and practical guidance. I responded warmly to their enthusiasm. Joyce Huggett, now a popular devotional writer, had attended our first conference in 1980. It was apparent then that she had a natural writing gift with an impressive contribution to make, drawing on her experience as a vicar's wife. Was there a new Joyce Huggett here this time, I wondered, who would become as widely known?

Authors are the life-blood of publishing. A good author deserves to be supported, honoured, recognised. For months, even years, they isolate themselves, researching, revising, reflecting, filling their waste-paper baskets. Charles Dickens wrote:

'It's only half an hour' – 'It's only an afternoon' – 'It's only an evening' – people say to me over and over again; but they don't know that it is impossible to commit one's self sometimes to any stipulated and set disposal of five minutes – or that the mere consciousness of an engagement will sometimes worry a whole day. These are the penalties paid for writing books. Whoever is devoted to an art must be content to deliver himself wholly up to it, and to find his recompense in it. I am grieved if you suspect me of not wanting to see you, but I can't help it: I must go my way whether or no.

During meals I was quizzed about bestsellers and publishing flops. My ego was boosted more by talking of the former. 'What was the biggest mistake you made?' I was asked over lunch one day. I thought of quite a few gaffes and confessed how I had missed the opportunity to publish for Joni Eareackson Tada when I was offered her first book by an American publisher. When it appeared year after year in the Christian books bestseller lists I wished I had considered it more carefully. When it was submitted I had been looking for British authors not a drama about a young American who had been severely handicapped in a tragic accident. Joni was a reminder of my fallibility.

I had been anticipating the lectures to be given by Marion Stroud and was not disappointed. She introduced her husband, Gordon, a dentist. Her first talk was practical, earthed in experience, for those in the early stages of writing. 'How can I make my manuscript have more editor appeal?' was the title.

Know your subject, she urged, target your audience, find out what other books exist in this subject area. Ask how is my proposed book different from them? Why am I particularly well qualified to write it? What research have I done? She told us to give space to thinking about the likely readers, where they live, what their occupation is, their spiritual status, leisure activities and hobbies. I found myself among those benefitting from the thoughtfulness of her well-prepared material.

Merrilyn Williams, who had known sunshine and shadow in her life, instructed us on writing biographical material. I scribbled down her advice:

Autobiography is not giving a day-to-day account of your life. Think of a patchwork, a quilt, a cushion-sized story. Find a theme which makes a statement about life, otherwise it will lack direction. Plot is the story-line that portrays the theme. The theme shouldn't be the problem but how it is overcome. The main theme may have underlying ones.

She told us of her own plotting. Present the initial problem, she advised. Who, what is it about? Name people. There should be emotion, dialogue, possible means of resolution; purpose that drives the actions and conflict in achieving resolution. Conflict, which is the heart of a good story, can be from the outside or the inside. The final outcome is concerned with if it will make it or not. The resolution must have a satisfactory answer which rings true.

Meanwhile Ann was reading manuscripts for me, counselling (as were other members of the resident community), and painting when she had the opportunity. Our room, however, was still troubling her:

> It is unbelievable that I can move from rejoicing in you to feeling downcast. My peace of mind depends on circumstances – not on you. I read about Paul and Silas in prison praising you.
>
> I feel tired after not sleeping well – noisy people overhead; annoyed at being in a room that is not very convenient for the speaker. Edward had fun opening his cards and presents for his sixty-second birthday – lingered over them. Hope he really likes them – he was pleased with the books – had wanted both he said. Please open the eyes of my heart to see you, Lord, to learn from you.

After breakfast on the Thursday I suggested to Merrilyn, Marion, Gordon and Ann that before the first lecture, which I was to give, we should meet for fifteen minutes in the chapel to pray. That gave me ten minutes first for a quick walk to gaze on the glorious views across the bay. The sea was a glittering silver. It was north Devon in its most amiable mood.

When the gong sounded for my lecture we swiftly left the quiet of the chapel, a place of sacred memories, for the lecture hall across the courtyard. Through the windows we could see it was comfortably full.

The session opened with worship conducted by the members of the community, mostly young, who had been assigned to support us that week. Many of them were giving a year or two to God before university or developing a career. As I took out my notes on the business-side of writing, I was hit by a severe pain across the back of my shoulders, followed by a tightness in my chest, along my arms. I thought of what had happened on the Downs.

'Dear Lord, please, not that. They're depending on me.'

Ann was going to leave after the worship to read a manuscript from one of the guests. 'Do you think you could fetch me two aspirin, please?' I whispered. 'There's water on the table.'

Suspecting a headache, she nodded and slipped out quietly, while the others stood to sing. I remained in my seat. Could I deliver a forty-five minute lecture? I knew the subject well enough, it was an easy talk in one sense, but the pain was intense. The aspirin should help.

Ann returned swiftly. 'No aspirin, but I found some paracetamol!' She whispered. 'Will you be all right?'

'With these, thanks, yes.' I didn't mention the back pain.

'See you at the coffee break.'

I reached for the water and swallowed the white tablets while everyone's eyes were closed.

'Bless Edward as he speaks to us, Lord, as he shares himself, his experience,' the worship leader prayed. I joined in the encouraging 'Amen'.

I placed my notes on the rostrum. The clock on the wall said 10.33. I was to conclude at 11.15 for the break. Forty-two minutes. I forced a confident smile and glanced at my first page.

'We've been singing about the Lord who prospers our work and defends us, which is apt as I'm talking about the business aspects of writing,' I said. I mentioned three Hodder authors who in the 1970s were earning in excess of £250,000 annually in royalties.

It was not particularly warm outside but I was getting uncomfortably hot, although my pain eased as the tablets took effect. 'Excuse me,' I muttered, pulling off my blue-striped pullover, a present from Ann. No one else seemed to be hot. I was perspiring.

I contrasted two authors who had achieved extraordinary success. One was my friend Dr Kenneth Taylor, who paraphrased *The Living Bible*. The other was the novelist, Alastair MacLean.

Dr Taylor could have been a millionaire. His *Living Bible* had sold in excess of 30 million copies. Instead he set up a charitable organisation into which his royalties were paid. Grants were made specifically for evangelism and some for social work including famine relief. Ken had barely changed his lifestyle since the publication of *The Living Bible*. On his most recent holiday in Britain with his wife Margaret they had stayed in low-priced bed-and-breakfast accommodation.

Alastair MacLean was brought up in a Scottish manse. He had trained as a school teacher. Ian and Margaret Chapman of Collins persuaded him to write his first book after reading his short story in the *Glasgow Herald*. That book was *HMS Ulysses*, which drew on the author's wartime experiences, and became a number one bestseller. It was followed by *The Guns of Navarone*, *Ice Station Zebra* and *Where Eagles Dare*. Alastair

MacLean gave up his job as a teacher in Glasgow, and tragically also cast aside the restraining influences of his Christian home. His road to fame and fortune led to personal misery, alcoholism and marriage breakdown. His life ended tragically in a Munich hospital.

I underlined the contrast between the two men. 'Don't make riches your aim,' I said, while acknowledging that in reality many authors received an hourly rate similar to that of an office cleaner, although the wealth for those like Jeffrey Archer, first published by Hodder, was immense.

The clock said 10.50. It was moving slowly. I had plenty to say, impossible to say it all, that would have taken several talks, ideally followed by questions, but I wanted to get out into the fresh air to cool off, to find a drink and a bed.

I took a publisher's contract and trudged through it clause by clause, highlighting what every author should know. 'Two copies of the complete contract shall be delivered . . . the published price shall be left to the sole discretion of the publisher . . . should the publisher sub-lease any of the volume rights they shall pay 50% of all monies received . . . the publisher shall pay an advance on account of all royalties . . . the publisher shall bear all expenses . . . if the work is allowed to go out of print . . . if any difference shall arise. . . .'

I explained what was meant by escalating royalties, unearned advances, option clauses, foreign and serial rights. They were important details for writers, a majority of those present, who did not have agents. I guessed many of them would have questions they would raise over lunch or supper or in the breaks. We didn't mind that; it was why we were there. We sat at different tables, hopefully with different people, for each meal, to give ample opportunity.

Five minutes to go. I could make it, although I was leaning heavily on the table, trusting no one sensed my discomfort. I did not hang around to see if they had. I was out of the door more quickly than I had entered it, heading into the main building, along the corridors to where drinks were served by the community. I'd be first in the queue, find a seat in a quiet spot and sit down. I'd recovered in that village church, no reason why I shouldn't now. I'd spend an hour this afternoon in bed, while Ann painted, ready for the teatime session. I had no inkling as I entered the building that I would leave it before lunch on a stretcher, attended by paramedics, accompanied by Ann.

My third lesson, of which I still have to remind myself, was:

I am not indispensable.

The Third Lesson

I AM NOT INDISPENSABLE

As for man, his days are as grass: as a flower of the field, so he flourisheth. For the wind passeth over it, and it is gone; and the place thereof shall know it no more.

—Psalm 103:15, 16 (AV)

I am sure that no one is indispensable, and that no one should try to be. David Sheppard tells in his charming book, *Parson's Pitch*, about a rector who paid a return visit to his old congregation. A lady met him and said, 'Oh, rector, the church has gone splendidly since you left!' And, you know, that was just about the greatest compliment she could have paid to a man's ministry. . . . A ministry after which there is a sag and collapse is essentially a failure.

—Dr William Barclay

You must remember to do less when you feel like doing more! We want and need you back. However, the kingdom of God will still come, even without our help! It's good for us to discover we're not indispensable – which makes it all the more gracious of the Lord to allow us the privilege of service.

—The Reverend J. David Pawson
(in a personal letter)

Chapter Four

Thursday 27 May, 2.20 pm

Here I am sitting in the intensive-care waiting room of
Barnstaple Hospital, with Edward rushed in with severe
chest pain and all I can think of is, Lord, please don't let him
die.

Now it's 2.45 pm and I was glad to be able to speak to
Helen at the office and eventually Julie (my sister) when I
got the number. I'm waiting to go in and see Edward and
writing this to stop myself from sitting and crying – seem to
have gone to pieces since I got here.

Lord, we are in your hands, but I do love him so much
and do want to keep him for a lot longer. It is strange what
I wrote after the parish weekend, 'Count it all joy when you
experience trials.'

When Edward was wheeled into intensive care I was
directed to the waiting room. It was terrible not to be with
him, not seeing him, not knowing what was happening.
There were several people there. I cried – they were all kind
– not fussing, just showing concern in their voices.

Then Frank came and told me his name and said that he'd
be looking after Edward. Said they were doing tests, X-rays,
etc, brought me a welcome cup of tea. Later came a smiling
(Dr) Steve Richardson, a friend of Janet Goodall, also a paediatrician; offered me a meal, shower, etc, that night and
said he'd be back.

As I telephoned my sister I saw the hills reflected in the mirror and thought of Psalm 121: 'My help cometh from the Lord,' and of Timothy Dudley Smith's lovely hymn, 'I lift my eyes to the quiet hills, in the press of a busy day; as green hills stand in a dusty land, so God is my strength and stay.'

It was a critical day, for Ann as well as me, an unforgettable Thursday, that would leave its imprint on the remainder of our earthly pilgrimage. We can hardly know of such events in advance, and for that we are grateful, but one is comforted by the knowledge that God knows, that nothing takes him by surprise.

After my lecture I had gone to the coffee point, a place of happy encounters, putting on a cheerful face. I was going to be well, to proceed normally, believing my discomfort should be put into perspective and forgotten.

I was a little discouraged when one of the guests, concern in his voice, asked, 'Have you ever had a heart attack?'

'Pardon?'

'Heart trouble? I wondered as you spoke.'

I knew the gentle questioner. A middle-aged man, in holiday attire, on his first visit to Lee Abbey, he had spent thirty minutes talking with me the previous day about his writing. What made him ask? He was not a doctor? I lifted the sugared coffee to my lips. It tasted good.

'I've been fortunate with my health,' I replied. 'Haven't been in hospital since I was nine. Appendicitis. I'm healthy enough, thanks.'

'Sorry, I shouldn't have asked,' he said graciously, walking away.

Marion Stroud approached briskly. She was purposeful in all she did. 'Thanks for the talk, Edward. Most helpful. I'd like to share part of it with the Fellowship of Christian Writers if you're willing.'

I glanced longingly at the cushioned bench. 'Marion, could we talk later?' An experienced speaker, she understood. 'Let's do that,' she agreed.

Someone else began talking to me, wanting advice. With relief I saw Ann approaching, coffee in hand, to ask how the session had gone. I realised I wasn't going to make Merrilyn's lecture, due to start in ten minutes, although I had a lot to learn from her.

'Ann, could you offer my apologies, I think I'll lie down for an hour.' Ann, the loving wife, looked at me. 'I'll come with you.'

Her decision to accompany me was to prove crucial.

Our trek began, Ann holding her coffee, a few paces behind me, upstairs, along several corridors until we reached ours, where I began to stagger. I steadied myself. Ann saw there was a problem. A serious one. There was no one else around, no telephones, everyone was in the coffee lounge, looking around the well-stocked bookroom or starting to make their way back for the next lecture.

As I stumbled on the bed, collapsing on the soft mattress, covering my face with my hands, there was an explosion of pain in my chest, in my back, down both arms. I thrashed around as Ann checked my pulse.

A heart attack, I told myself, but didn't mouth the words. Ann no doubt knew. I was unaware that a quarter of a million people in Britain die from them annually, a large percentage in the first fifteen minutes. It was grim enough without being aware of the statistics.

'I'll ask the office to phone the doctor. They'll call an ambulance,' Ann explained, her voice calm, her heart trembling.

'You're not going to leave me? Don't,' I wanted to say, and perhaps I did, but I knew I must reach the hospital. Very quickly. The pain was unbearable.

'I'll call Mary from the lecture hall. She'll phone, so I can hurry back.' Mary and her husband, Walter, were doctors and had been sharing actively in the group sessions.

I saw Ann leave the bedroom with dismay, but she had no choice. My chest was being squeezed in an iron clamp as she raced along the corridors, down the stairs, across the courtyard. I have never felt so alone. 'I can't take much more, Lord. Let them get an ambulance soon.'

With the rest of the nation I had watched medical programmes on television. Emergency ambulances had cardiac life-saving equipment; hospital spelt safety: a special unit, oxygen, drugs, monitors, specialists. But where was the hospital? Not in Lynton or Lynmouth, and nowhere on Exmoor across which we had travelled on Monday. In visits to Lee Abbey over thirteen years we had never seen one. At home there was the Kent and Sussex twenty minutes away and a cottage hospital within walking distance.

Three weeks before I had been the speaker at a men's breakfast in the Winston Manor Hotel in Crowborough. It had attracted, as usual, almost as many men on the fringe of the Church, or outside it, as regular worshippers. In my talk I had suggested that life was like a book. When we are born all the pages are blank. Each of us has some idea of how many chapters of our story have been written but even the smartest cannot predict how many remain. Some of us might be half way through, some may have reached the final chapter, the last page. Looking around at the relaxed men, there was happily none who appeared about to make his final exit, yet what I said was true. I added that a Christian, in non-theological terms, was someone who had invited Jesus Christ to be his Lord and Saviour, who had asked Christ to step into his story to direct the writing of the remaining pages. A non-Christian was someone who claimed he could write his story without assistance, who rejected God's help.

Crying for Ann's return, I wondered if I had reached the last page, the final paragraph? My own death had not previously come within my field of vision.

But my thoughts, increasingly incoherent and scrambled, were not primarily of death but of pain. The agony was almost unbearable. And I was not brave. If only I had taken the precaution of going to hospital on Saturday, of talking to our GP. An ECG, a blood pressure test, routine procedures, freely available. What a fool. What a price.

As Ann opened the door into the lecture room, Dr Mary was a few feet away. Ann beckoned her. 'Edward has severe chest pains. He's in our room!' she burst out.

Walter joined them and together they hurried upstairs, three competent doctors, on holiday, but without the instruments of their profession or the medication. Walter took one look at me, knowing instantly what was wrong, and made for the office phone.

Mary felt my pulse, then prayed. It was a prayer of faith, a cry to God from a medic who knew precisely what was happening, who was confident that God could intervene. In her eyes, God and the medical profession were in partnership. She concluded her prayer with a request that I would be filled with faith and not fear.

'I have no fear,' I managed to protest, and it was partly true, 'but I need to get to hospital.'

'You'll soon be there, Edward. And now Ann, will you pray?'

Ann had not ceased praying, more earnestly than ever, but with Mary's encouragement she found the ordered words to go with her silent cry to God.

'Thank you, Lord, that all his life Edward has trusted

you, known you, loved you.' She gripped my hand. 'And thank you that he still trusts you now.' There flashed into her mind a picture of the strong arms of the Lord upholding, supporting me. And the words of the Psalmist, 'Underneath are the everlasting arms.'

Walter hurried in. 'I got through to the surgery. The doctor was out on his calls. The receptionist said she'd be able to contact him and he'd come directly.'

Would it be soon enough? The unspoken question hung in the air. There was not the slightest let-up in the level of pain, each minute seemed an eternity. Mary, always practical, slipped downstairs to collect Ann's bag where she had left it with the manuscript she had been reading for me.

Tony, a Lee Abbey chaplain, with another staff member, knocked on the door. I dimly heard him say the surgery, unable to locate the doctor, had phoned for the ambulance. They had accepted Walter's diagnosis, his sense of urgency.

'It's on its way from Barnstaple,' Tony confirmed.

Barnstaple? That was a journey of twenty-two miles, along winding Devon country roads, where one was as likely to meet a herd of cows as another vehicle. Was that the best they could do?

Unexpectedly, happily, the doctor arrived. A red-faced, bearded man, he responded rapidly, opening his bag and giving intravenous morphine to dull the pain, asking few questions.

With the attention of four doctors, and the morphine, the iron grip on my chest eased, and I was distinctly drowsy when the paramedics arrived and carried me down to the rear exit. An oxygen mask assisted my breathing. They attached a drip and various monitors. Their warm, West Country voices, their kindness reassured me.

'They'll be waiting for us at the hospital. It's one of the finest. Quite new. You'll be well looked after there.'

They had arrived more quickly than expected and had parked a few yards from the lecture hall. Fortunately, the guests were facing away from the courtyard. Merrilyn alone would be able to see the ambulance and she would have no idea it was me.

The attendant told Ann where to sit, pointing out the seat belt. She clung to hastily gathered toilet items, pyjamas, a dressing gown, nothing for herself.

I became agitated by the oxygen mask after a few miles, so a nasal catheter was produced as we speeded along the narrow roads, fresh green hedgerows on either side. Ann mentioned occasional glimpses of the sea, between the low hills. She thought of her one moment of relief in the last hour – when she noticed there was no hole in the toe of the socks I was wearing. Later, she would laugh about it.

I drifted off.

'Is that the hospital?' I heard her question.

'A couple of minutes,' the attendant said.

Ann saw the words 'Devon and District Hospital' as we drew into a modern complex surrounded by low hills and rich green fields, on the Lee Abbey side of Barnstaple. I was too fuzzy to notice the impressive entrance but was aware of being hurried into a lift on a trolley and admitted to the coronary care unit. A team of doctors and nurses, competent voices, another drip, oxygen, an ECG monitor. 'The masks give more support than the catheter,' the nurse insisted. When I opened my eyes again the cardiologist, two doctors and the sister were conferring by the window. I couldn't hear their conversation and I didn't want to.

Although some chest pain remained, overwhelming relief had replaced the persistent agony. Nowhere would

I be better cared for than in this specialist unit, with the latest technology and drugs, watched over by a loving God. When the Psalmist wrote, 'Even though I walk through the valley of the shadow of death you are with me,' he could not have visualised these facilities, but I clung to the truth of the familiar words. I had watched others journey through this valley to the city of eternal light, which had 'no need of sun or moon to shine upon it, for the glory of the Lord is its light'.

I have no memory of the next two hours but someone must have replaced my trousers and shirt with the pyjamas Ann had brought from Lee Abbey. I was heavily sedated and when I became aware of my surroundings it was only hazily: some equipment, a table, chairs, a basin, a lot of lights. Frank, a male nurse, was checking again that I had no other physical problems, was on no regular medication. I hoped it was he who had removed my clothes and not one of the pretty nurses. I didn't ask.

My watch had been removed from my wrist: my most important accessory. My muzzy thoughts were still conference-centred. I guessed the regular afternoon walk would be taking place now, a gentle stroll, involving a bit of a climb, lasting an hour or so, and normally led by a community member. We sometimes joined it. I knew I would not be speaking at the conference again but harboured a silly hope of returning to Sussex by car in a couple of days, sharing the driving with Ann. I was not thinking clearly, life had become all confusion, and I drifted off.

When Ann was allowed in again she sat by the bed loosely holding my hand, wondering if there would be a future together. She squeezed it gently when my eyes opened. I turned my head. She gave me that warm tender smile that melted my heart on St Valentine's Day 1977, when I proposed to her sitting in the car on the main road outside St Helier Hospital, in South London. Red double-decker buses, lorries and cars sped by, but we barely noticed. It was a romantic day, an unromantic setting. The traffic hadn't troubled us, we might have been on a desert island.

Ann had been on call as the registrar in the maternity ward all weekend so she had been weary when I collected her for an early dinner in a Reigate hotel. The large restaurant was almost deserted, not very welcoming. I could see the tiredness in her eyes. She explained that there had been emergency calls to the labour ward several times each night after long demanding days caring for expectant mothers seeing new babies into the world. When conversation flagged I talked to her of some notable women authors: the sprightly Commissioner Catherine Bramwell Booth of the Salvation Army; Jackie Pullinger, and Mrs Martin Luther King, who astonished us with a wonderful solo at a lunch we gave to mark the publication of her book *My Life with Martin Luther King*. I encouraged her to talk about the patients and staff in the Thai hospital where she had served. She took ages to choose her dessert, each one looking so appetising. The choice up country in Thailand had been more limited.

I took her back to St Helier's at 9.15 pm, but just before we drove into the grounds I pulled the car into the kerb. It wasn't a premeditated act, rather a reluctance to separate, to let her go. I hated returning home to find no lights on in the windows as I turned into our cul-de-sac. She tells me she never actually said yes to my proposal but her beautiful smile was her eloquent response. When my first wife, Gwen, died of cancer, I thought I would never know true happiness again but with that smile I found it.

Since our wedding in 1977 we had travelled widely together meeting authors, publishers and booksellers in America, South Africa, Singapore, Hong Kong and Bangkok. But the highlight for me had been when she took me to the hospital at Manorom and we stayed in the house on stilts, surrounded by paddy fields, in which she had once lived. One didn't need central heating and the fan went all night.

I never thought I would be pleased to be lying in a hospital bed but I was now.

'How do you feel darling? No sorry, you don't have to talk.'

I wanted to reach out and take her in my arms and kiss her, but I couldn't move and dare not take off the mask. I was not in a position to support, or comfort.

'The pain's eased, thanks. But what's happened to me, to us, what's it going to mean? How long will I be here?'

'I don't know. You're in good hands. Leave it to the doctors.' There were footsteps outside but no one entered.

'It's the church prayer meeting tonight. I've phoned Andrew, at the vicarage, they'll be praying. I talked to Helen at the office. She was shocked, sent her love, said they would pray.'

'Tell my family in Sheffield please, but ask them not to come. I won't be in here long enough. But they should know. Perhaps my brother Norman should tell Mother.'

She was ushered outside. A further examination, more consultations. Later, I think a doctor, it may have been a nurse, told me they wished to inject an expensive clot-busting drug.

'It's most effective if given within four hours of a heart attack. It will dissolve the clot, allowing the blood to flow freely.'

'That's good.'

'It's a comparatively new drug. There's a very slight risk of a stroke, really tiny, but you should know as you have the right to refuse it.'

A stroke? I thought of my Father in his last year, helpless by the fireside, dribble running down his chin, unable to do anything, totally dependent, after a stroke. Because I loved him I wanted him to die, to be released from the indignity.

'And if I don't have it?'

'For the next few hours the risks are greater. On balance, we recommend it.'

'I'll take your advice. Thank you for the warning.'

As the drug was injected I reassured myself – the risk was really tiny.

Steve, the paediatrician, had returned. He and his wife Elaine invited Ann to their home, a few minutes from the hospital, and hoped she would join them for a meal and stay with them as long as she wished. It was an act of kindness, quite overwhelming, from a family we had never met.

The endless day drew to a close, although, in Ann's words, I was 'blotto' for much of it. The oxygen mask, the drip and monitors remained but the pain had gone. Movement was still restricted on both sides by the tubes and leads when Ann kissed me goodnight.

In my half-conscious state I relived my lecture, the struggle to our room, the wait for the ambulance, the knowledge that I had been a heartbeat from heaven. Indeed still was.

How abruptly this life can end. How little thought we normally give to it, to our ultimate destination. Many spend more thought on planning their summer holiday. My fourth lesson was surely:

Be ready for departure.

The Fourth Lesson

BE READY FOR DEPARTURE

Death is the destiny of every man;
the living shall take this to heart.
Moreover, no man knows when his hour will come.
—Ecclesiastes 7:2;9:12 (NIV)

When a man in his fifties mutters, 'I'm not as young as I used to be' he may be looking both backwards and forwards, mourning the decline of his previous powers and acknowledging that decline will continue. Yet he is unlikely to face the obvious end-point which, of course, is his death. Most of us find it hard, if not impossible to conceive of our own death.
—Althea Pearson, Growing through Loss and Grief

The last thing you want to do is the last thing you will do.
—Anonymous

Many of the people who plan to become Christians at the eleventh hour unfortunately die at 10.30.
—Pam Weaver

A large proportion of deaths occur without any preparation as far as the outsider or relative can tell. The person has seemed in good health, or perhaps there may have been minor symptoms which have been ignored or treated with simple medicines. And then, apparently without warning, death occurs. . . . Often these unexpected deaths are thought to be the consequence of a sudden, painless, heart attack, and we feel that would be the ideal way of 'going'. They do underline the need for people to be prepared, however, and not to leave things to be sorted out 'when we have the time'.
—Anthony M. Smith, Gateway to Life

Chapter Five

Thank you, Lord, that Edward is stable and not in pain now
– please care for him, watch over him. This room is quiet
and I'm glad to be near Edward. It's been a strange day,
trying to get everyone on the phone, having to rush out
again because his heart rate was up; then Tony, the chaplain, and Mary coming to take me out for Ryvita and soft
drinks in the grounds, and no sooner back with Edward
than Steve offering to take me home for a meal – and I
wanted to get back.

Elaine gave me flowers. She offered me a shower or bath,
had a lovely fluffy towel, little bag of toothpaste, brush, etc.
I did feel much better after food and a shower.

The office got through to the vicarage and Andrew
phoned back and was a dear. He said they'd be praying
tonight.

Oh dear, this morning seems a long time away. Don't
know why I feel I must write it all down. Edward had a
heart attack, myocardial infarction, and has a lignocaine
drip. Had TPA (like Streptokinase only better). He mentioned the doctor had said there was a slight risk of a stroke
but bigger risk if not taken. Glad I didn't know.

I feel as if I've never been with him, now am nearby, did
have an hour or so – interrupted by Mike Edson the
warden of Lee Abbey and his wife Frances, who came over

to see us and prayed. Seems all these kind people have taken me away from Edward but thank you for sending them Lord, and for all the support and your arms enfolding me.

Please help me to sleep.

Ann was awake around 2 am. A nurse gave her a flask of water, milk and coffee, and said I was awake. Would she like to see me?

'Didn't know you were still here,' I said softly, when the door opened, reassured by her presence.

'You've forgotten. I told you last night. I've got a comfortable bed next door. I hope you've slept.'

It was heartening to know that Ann was within call, a few paces away, could be with me in seconds. Yet she needed to sleep, after all the trauma and not knowing what tomorrow might hold.

'I dozed off, now I'll go back to sleep more happily. You're not so pale, got more colour in your cheeks. Look brighter,' she said.

'I am. But I'm worried that if I die you won't know how to sort out our affairs. It's all in my desk at home. My mind isn't functioning properly, but in the morning can you bring a notepad and paper and I'll explain.'

I'd been responsible for paying bills, arranging standing charges, checking bank statements, looking after savings accounts. A few items were kept at another address – one Saturday afternoon there had been a break-in at home and we had become cautious.

'Don't think about dying. But I'll bring in the paper and pen.' She was silent for a moment. 'Are you afraid you might die?'

For fifteen hours we had lived with the possibility without discussing it. We both knew these were crucial hours which was why I was being so carefully monitored, why the nurse looked in constantly, even though my heart and pulse were being monitored on the screen on her desk outside.

'I'm ready, if I die. Apart from giving you that list. And I need to tell you about the business.' I could see the brave resolve on her face – she would not let me see her cry. She bent to give me another goodnight kiss. I closed my eyes as she left.

'If I die, please take care of Ann, Lord. Please.'

I recalled my anguish, my darkness, when Gwen died on that cold March morning, never to see the new border burst into bloom which we had planted in autumn. I knew all about the anger and the distress of the partner who is left.

There was the dark chilly Sunday evening when I drove to Tonbridge, parked the car, and walked along its High Street, past the ancient castle and across the river, desolate, bewildered like a child. Amiable, open-hearted friends gave unstinting support. I was invited to phone them at any hour and did. What a debt I owed to three or four of them. In the dim light of intensive care, sur-rounded by shadows, I longed to save Ann from such heartbreak.

And there were regrets, too, many of them. Sins for-given, but not forgotten, which still haunted me. If I could begin life and start again. But would I do better? And the grim realisation that I probably wouldn't. Yet I had no fear of meeting God, believing in his mercy. Christ died for me. Around 5 am I began to look for Ann. Happily she was still sleeping.

During the coming day she sat with me, watching, waiting, while I drifted between awareness and oblivion. She took out her journal: 'In all you have done for me in the last few months, Lord Jesus, have you been preparing me for this? Please God, not for his death now – I don't know how to cope with the thought much less the reality.'

The oxygen mask was an annoyance. I protested in vain that it added to my difficulties.

'Doctor's orders,' the nurse smiled. The uniform, the place, gave her authority. I watched the monitor and as the day passed saw it settle to a more regular pattern.

Bad news travels swifter than Concorde. The cards and flowers were already arriving, reminders we were being prayed for, and Ann savoured every one. She arranged the flowers and reread the cards. For some reason, quite unforgivable, I refused to look at them, had no interest, asked her not to put them round the bed. Indeed, I wished they hadn't come. She was puzzled. So was I.

'They show how much you're loved. That's what they're saying. You should be grateful.'

'I don't want to be loved. I want to be better.'

'They must have rushed to the post box the moment they heard. Look at this beautiful one.'

To please her, I looked for a second, then asked her to put them out of sight in the locker. They were written confirmation, evidence on paper that I'd had a heart attack. I wanted life to go on as normal, not to be surrounded by these visual reminders that I had changed.

Ann couldn't fathom my response, so I promised to read them all when I arrived home, little realising by then I would be grateful for every one, and for the flowers. Now they were invading my private world. I wished to keep the knowledge within a tight circle, I was too ill, too frail to cope with the sentiments expressed. Let me hole up in an inaccessible place until I was well again.

If I had been less selfish, acknowledging the cards were for Ann as well as myself, I would have said put them up, visible reminders of those at home. She needed to see them in her dark moments.

The thought that I was the subject of phone calls between friends, and whispered conversations in the high street and supermarket, was as awful as the cards. I could almost hear them.

'He's the age for problems like that. Women get cancer, men have heart attacks.'

'Yes, dear, I read in the newspaper that one quarter of all heart attacks occur before a man retires. One quarter. That they're responsible for forty per cent of deaths among men between forty-five and sixty-four.'

Stop talking about me. Forget you've been told. Please don't tell anyone else.

The nurse bustled in.

'The Bishop of Southampton telephoned to ask how you were. He was really concerned. He sends his love to you and Ann, said he and his wife were praying for you.'

In spite of myself I was grateful that he had made the time.

'Who do you think told him, Ann?'

'Someone probably phoned from Lee Abbey, knowing we'd been there when he was the Warden.'

'The nurse probably thinks I'm a clergyman!'

'I brought the notepad,' Ann said when I had slept a little. 'For your list. Do you want to tell me now?'

'I was worried in the night that if I died, until the will was sorted out, you might run short of cash. There's an instant withdrawal account at the Woolwich. Enough to pay the household bills for several months, in addition to what's in our current bank account.'

'Are there bills to be paid?'

'No, nothing. The council tax is on a monthly standing order. The water rates are paid until October. I settled the Access card before we came.'

'I'd ask David for advice.' David was our accountant, a Christian.

'He knows about the business, the agency, the magazines. Carol Lewry signs the office cheques and pays them. There's no overdraft or loans. With Carol, Wallace, Penny, Jane and the others, the office can carry on for months until matters are sorted out.'

During the next twelve hours I added to the list. Doing so gave me, if not Ann, some peace. I needed to know I had done everything possible, that there would be no unpleasant surprises, no practical problems, that with a few words I might have easily resolved. As I had left all matters concerning the kitchen and the house in Ann's hands, so she had left the bank statements and bills in mine. We had a joint account but she rarely looked at it. I was fortunate, I reflected bleakly. A younger man in my situation would have had the worry of a mortgage, how a wife and children might survive.

'Ann, the dog's due to be collected on Sunday and the cat on Monday morning. Go home tomorrow. I'll follow on the train as soon as I can. Sooner if possible.'

She shook her head.

'I'm not going home without you. I phoned Eric, next door. He'll feed the goldfish, cancel the milk, keep an eye on the house. You're not to worry about anything. The dog and the cat can stay where they are. I'll ring the kennels and the cattery. I'm not leaving you here.'

Ann had phoned her friend, Ruth Fowke, in Guildford, with whom she had trained at medical school in Cardiff. Ruth was special to both of us. She had introduced Ann to me and I had published for her. She had recently retired as a consultant psychiatrist but still led a full life, advising missionary societies, working with Inter Health, serving on committees. She was often away from home at weekends speaking at conferences, but this was a bank holiday.

'Ann, I'm coming. I know the road. You need someone with you,' Ruth said.

'But Ruth, it's an awful long way and the roads will be

busy for the holiday weekend. But it would be marvellous,' Ann replied, engulfed by her generosity. 'Are you sure?'

'I'll find somewhere to stay when I arrive. Leave that to me. Don't worry.'

Visitors, other than Ann, had not been permitted into intensive care to see me but, being a doctor, Ruth gained access when she arrived that evening. She was impressed with the technology, some equipment so new that she had not seen it before.

'Well, Edward, you've chosen a great place to get well in,' she beamed. She asked the staff to explain some of it to her. 'You mean, this machine actually takes his pulse automatically every fifteen minutes?'

'Day and night, so there's no need to wake. We can see it on the desk outside.'

Warm-hearted Steve and Elaine invited Ruth to join Ann and sleep in their home. My condition was sufficiently stable for Ann to go there that night and her doing so reassured me. She fell asleep reasonably quickly but soon after dawn was reaching for her Bible and journal.

When I woke up I was thinking heart attack, he's had a coronary, an MI – all reeling round in my mind. I've never seen someone with coronary before – his face as he lay on the bed, pale, shocked, rolling around in pain, but I could sit by him, hold his hand, but not do much more except pray for him.

'Lord Jesus, keep Edward in your care.' Mary prayed and asked me if I'd like to. I asked you to hold him in your arms, to feel your love as he had all his life – I stumbled on 'life' thinking maybe this was the end of it.

The ambulance men were very kind and chatted calmly, yet got on with putting a long plastic lead to his finger to monitor oxygen.

63

It must be nearly 7 am. I can't go back to sleep so I'll creep downstairs for a cup of coffee and read through the cards again; and Andrew's two lovely letters, one to Edward and one to me. He was very dear on the phone – said he'd like to give me a hug, consider myself hugged – well, I've had a lot of hugs.

The nurse brought me a little breakfast, my first food for forty-eight hours. She propped my head up with pillows. Later, she suggested a bedbath. I turned pale.

'Could my wife do it, please?' I stuttered. I didn't quite know what a bedbath involved, but didn't like the thought of anyone doing it except Ann.

'Of course,' she smiled, understandingly.

Ann readily agreed, when she and Ruth arrived. Ruth left us, firmly closing the door behind her.

'It's good to have her here,' Ann said, reaching for the water, soap and flannel. 'I'll be grateful for the rest of my life. Someone to talk to about ordinary things! She pulled back the sheets. 'She's brought a touch of normality to what otherwise seems an unpleasant dream.'

I was given permission to remove the oxygen mask, leaving it by my head on the pillow in case of need, and I was also disconnected from one of the monitors. Having been flat on my back for two days and nights I could now roll over onto my side, sympathising with those who did not have this option, sometimes for months. Ordinary things, done unthinkingly, were now seen as privileged. Ann combed what little hair I had. I didn't ask for a mirror but felt more cheerful, more like myself.

For a few minutes. Until Ann and Ruth went out for a coffee break.

I tried to sit up a little, placing my hands on the mattress to give myself leverage. I pushed. I called on all my strength to move up the pillow. And achieved nothing.

64

Until that moment I did not know I had lost the strength in my limbs. I made another fruitless attempt. I might as well have been strapped down. I could barely move myself and was alarmed. Where had all my natural energy gone? It was only a week since I had been walking the South Downs. I was facing a great chasm.

Like a lightning flash the physical consequences of a heart attack hit me. I was not the person who had arrived at Lee Abbey earlier in the week, who had stood and lectured on what publishers looked for. My thought of sharing the driving with Ann on the journey home from hospital was fantasy, also that of returning to the office in a week or two. What a burden, what an embarrassment I was going to be. To others, to myself.

I was struggling with tears when Ann opened the door followed by Ruth. One quick look and Ruth withdrew. A man does not like to be seen with overflowing eyes. We are the braver, stronger, warrior sex, aren't we? Ann came alongside, her face melted into tenderness.

'What's wrong, love? You're making good progress. Do you have a pain? Is there something I can do for you?'

'I can't sit up.' I wiped my eyes. 'There's no power in my arms, my back, I'm as helpless as a baby. No one told me I'd be as frail as this, with no strength in my arms, my back. I was able to reach our room at Lee Abbey – I was walking then. Now I can't lift myself up.'

'You've had a heart attack. It's a consequence. It's temporary. Each day you'll regain some strength as your heart recovers. You'll do more and more. It won't always be like this and you'll be surprised by the progress. They'll have you out of bed in a couple of days.' She bent to kiss me, realising as she did so how any weakness would also affect her, yet concealing her concern. 'You'll need to be patient – we both will.' I wasn't sure I was very good at being patient, or wanted to learn.

So this was the price of an addiction to a busy life, perhaps of eating a wrong diet from boyhood, of not adequately exercising, of driving instead of walking, of too many hours at my desk, too few in the garden? Had my constant tiredness in the past year been a sign? Or would it have happened anyway in the way people in some families seem to get cancer or back problems? I had no answers.

I should have asked Ruth about the tiredness. She had written and lectured on how chronic fatigue means we are only half alive much of the time.

The biblical view is not a choice between work and leisure, but a balance. After each burst of work in creation God rested, and reviewed what he had done. After half a dozen periods of work he took a longer break. Work and leisure together give a complementary rhythm to life. They are creation ordinances.

Saturday 29 May 1993 was a grey day whatever the weather. There was not only the damaged heart muscle but some unexpected news. Ruth brought in a copy of *The Daily Telegraph*. I had no desire to read it or anything else, although I normally enjoyed the Weekend section if we switched for the day from *The Times*. She opened the paper out and pointed to a news story. It contained a second blow. I read it almost with disbelief. 'It can't be true,' I wanted to shout. 'It's a denial of all the promises of the past.'

The story was a further pointer to what had been a secure, unchanging world collapsing around me, an indicator of what in the coming months would be my rather harsh fifth lesson:

Don't cling to the past.

The Fifth Lesson

DON'T CLING TO THE PAST

But one thing I do: Forgetting what is behind and straining towards what is ahead, I press on towards the goal to win the prize for which God has called me heavenwards in Christ Jesus.

—Philippians 3:13 (NIV)

There are people who are still prisoners of some adventure in the past. Ten or twenty years ago it was really an adventure, one so thrilling that now they are not letting go of it – though it is grown quite old – for fear of losing their treasure and falling back into the voice of a mediocre existence. They cling to it and so deprive themselves of that constant resurgency of adventure which characterises life. There is, then, a necessary rhythm between engagement and disengagement if the instinct of adventure is to be able to develop.

—Dr Paul Tournier, The Adventure of Living

Chapter Six

It was the most unexpected publishing story in a decade. Hodder and Stoughton, to which I had been linked as an editor, director and literary agent for more than twenty-five years, was being taken over by Headline Publishing. If Cardinal Basil Hume had been appointed Archbishop of Canterbury, if Billy Graham had become the Pope, if Margaret Thatcher had joined the Labour Party, I could not have been more astounded.

A family firm, which boasted of its independence, and was loved by its authors because of it, a highly regarded company that considered good books more significant than maximising profits, had sold out.

When the Dean of St Paul's Cathedral had prayed at the opening of a new head office for Hodder he had quoted the Old Testament words: 'Except the Lord build the house their labour is lost that build it; except the Lord keep the city the watchman waketh but in vain.' Now the house had been sold. There may have been excellent economic reasons, even pressing financial ones, but the loyal long-serving staff would feel betrayed.

Hodder and Stoughton had been founded in 1868 by two Christian businessmen, and I had been involved under Leonard Cutts, a distinguished editor and director, in arranging events to mark its centenary in Stationers' Hall, London. A highlight was an exhibition of religious books, opened by the Lord Mayor of London. The chairman, Paul Hodder-Williams, said, 'Hodder and Stoughton's one hundred years of Christian publishing began and continues under a sense of vocation. . . . Within our Christian conviction therefore we hope never to reject the eternal gospel and its living literature.' Religious publishing 'was not a mere department of Hodder and Stoughton, but the inspiration of the firm's total purpose,' wrote John Attenborough, the joint chief executive.

'What do you know about Headline?' Ann asked, seeing my consternation.

'Very little, recently founded I think, probably dynamic, but with no known commitment to Christian books. I can't believe it, Ann. Can they be trusted with the *New International Bible*? I worked so hard over seven years to secure the rights for Hodder. And since I left I've given Hodder the best of my agency authors – more than sixty of them. They'll have read this story and be trying to reach me on the phone.'

'I'm not worried about the authors, or Hodders, I'm worried about you,' Ann protested. 'Don't get worked up about it now. You can do that later when you're stronger.'

'I know, but I'm dumbfounded. Some of the staff have spent almost a lifetime there.'

When Ann and Ruth had gone out for a meal, I asked the nurse how soon I could return to the office. For the sake of the Hodder authors on my list it was urgent.

'Open your mouth please,' she replied, putting the thermometer in. After a pause, 'With most patients it's about three months. It can be a little less, or more. Ask the doctor when you see him in the morning.'

Three months? I didn't pursue the conversation when the thermometer was removed. In a couple of days I would demonstrate how quickly I was getting back to normal and then ask the doctor. I never took a holiday of more than two weeks, I couldn't be spared. I turned my head to the monitor which recorded my pulse. It had fluctuated between 60 and 150 with no activity on my part but was now recording a steady 90–91. I was doing well.

When Ann and Ruth disappeared that evening for Steve and Elaine's home they were as cheerful as a couple of medical students on a night out, and their cheerfulness was an encouragement to me, offering more reassurance about my progress. Ann was laughing, enjoying Ruth's stimulating companionship.

Sleep did not come easily that night. When with difficulty I was able to put the shock of Hodder out of my mind I worried about my inability to sit up that morning. My longing was to reach the bathroom unaided – or even with assistance.

After midnight a raucous voice outside intensive care persisted until I could cope no longer. The night nurses were female and this was a loud threatening voice, most certainly not the doctor's. Heading towards frenzy, I pressed the buzzer for the nurse, who appeared at once.

'Could you get hospital security?' I asked, unreasonably. Alarm appeared on her face. 'That loud non-stop voice outside. It's not what the doctor ordered. It's gone on and on. I can't sleep.'

'I'm sorry,' she said, her face white. 'Leave it with me.' I did not hear another word. Had it been an unoccupied porter, an aggressive boyfriend, an intruder from another ward? It didn't matter. Silence followed and I fell asleep.

On Sunday morning I was cheered when, with little

assistance I was able to sit up for breakfast, pillows piled high behind.

'We may be moving you to Trinity ward at lunch-time,' the nurse said. 'It's a pleasant small bay with eight beds. All men. You'll see the same doctors but have different nurses.'

I didn't want to go. I felt secure, protected, sheltered where I was, but the bed was needed and I was informed it was the first step towards going home. Ann and Ruth had gone to church with Steve, Elaine and their two young children. I listened to the church bells and thought of All Saints at home where, no doubt, I would be included in the public prayer for those who were in hospital. I trusted they would pray for Ann too.

Trinity ward. I liked the name. With my odds and ends from the locker, dressing gown, slippers, medical notes, and the flowers from my nephew, David and his wife Sue, the porter pushed me along. 'In the name of the Father, Son and Holy Spirit go with me,' I prayed. A nurse walked alongside chatting.

The cheery porter, watching that nothing fell off the trolley, muttered my name aloud, 'Edward England,' with a broad West Country accent. 'It's you who've kept us on the go in the post room. There's been as many cards, letters, flowers for you as for the rest of the hospital.'

No doubt an exaggeration but my mind was on our destination. Trinity made me think of hushed cloisters, gowned figures, ancient music, well-preserved stone walks. When I was wheeled in I saw at once that it was not like that. Patients glanced from behind Sunday papers, phones were ringing at the nurses' desk, visitors were clutching plastic bags with biscuits, grapes, choco-lates. After the quietness since Thursday I was threat-ened by the noise. I didn't belong; I didn't want to.

'Quiet everyone,' I wanted to shout, but being a coward, and recognising their rights, I pulled the bedclothes higher.

'Plenty for you to watch and hear,' Ruth said thinking positively when they returned from church.

'It's awful,' I whispered, pushing myself up on the pillow to talk to them.

'You've sat up without help,' Ann laughed. 'You must be pleased.'

'Tell me about the service. Was it a good sermon?'

'Be honest, Ann,' urged Ruth.

'I dozed off,' she confessed. 'Unknowingly. And that's no reflection on the sermon. Shows I was comfortable and relaxed about you. All I can remember is the preacher saying that our disappointments are his appointments, that all things work together for good to those who love God.'

'We just passed two bays which are reserved for women,' Ruth said. 'They're filled with flowers, cards, fruit.' She looked at this bay. 'Why have the men hidden theirs?' No patient had more than one card on his locker.

'You can put up the card you gave me Ann. With David and Sue's flowers,' I said.

'What about this one? Signed by everyone at Thursday night's prayer meeting including all your staff even those from other churches. Andrew must have been surprised to see them.'

I looked at the names, heartened by their affection. I nodded, handing it back. Ann beamed. A modest victory. 'I'll treasure it,' I said.

'And one from the bank manager?' She was pushing hard.

'No.'

The previous day, while I'd slept, Ruth had driven Ann to Lee Abbey to collect our car which had been left there.

It was a larger car than Ann normally drove, an automatic, and she was relieved that Ruth followed closely behind along the country roads. Going back also enabled her to say goodbye to the caring Community members. She told her diary:

> I'm almost afraid to believe Edward's so much better and worry he's covering up. It was good to see Lee Abbey and erase all the awful memories – to see the place where Edward had stood talking to Marion. When I packed, Mary came with me, the room was tidy, the bed made, and I didn't have time to think about Edward rolling on it in dreadful pain. Mary has been so good.
>
> At the hospital his shaving went well. I lathered, he shaved – only two cuts! It was good to be able to do something for him. I'm almost afraid to trust his improvement, Lord. Help me to be myself, to cope well with these coming days. I feel so much better, it's only now I'm beginning to realise how stunned I was.

Someone gave me a Sunday paper with another story about the upheaval in the publishing world. Thirty-nine-year-old Tim Hutchinson, a founding member of Headline, would be the chief executive of the enlarged company to be called Hodder Headline. It made sense to put Hodder with its long tradition first. He promised comprehensive changes to 'increase efficiency and profitability and to create growth'. Headline had consistently achieved substantial sales and profit growth since its establishment in 1986.

The publishing world, in Britain and America, had been undergoing a revolution with men like Robert Maxwell and Rupert Murdoch including books in their media companies alongside newspapers and television stations. These conglomerates paid enormous royalty advances to a handful of authors, particularly novelists, while sometimes dropping established writers of quality.

I was uneasy about how Hodder authors would fare and the staff. Perhaps unnecessarily.

But the page one story that day was not about Hodder Headline but about Michael Heseltine, the energetic sixty-year-old President of the Board of Trade, who, it was said, wanted to be Prime Minister. He was in hospital following a heart attack while on holiday in Venice. He had been transported there by boat.

He was a prime example of the driven man, with widespread business interests, as well as a political career. He had collapsed on a 'romantic weekend' with his wife in the best hotel in Venice. His doctor told reporters: 'Heart attacks occur unannounced at any time.'

There was a column of gloomy figures. The death rate from coronaries in Britain was among the highest in the world. While mortality rates had fallen in America by 55% since 1970, the comparative figure for England, Wales and Northern Ireland was 24%. In 1992, 48,623 men and 39,211 women had died in this manner.

First reports indicated that Heseltine's heart attack was not too serious. By the autumn he might be back in Westminster, but his chances of ever taking up the occupancy of 10 Downing Street were reduced.

I had warmed to the kidney patient in the opposite bed. During the evening he regaled us with stories of how he spent a typically restricted day, mostly confined to his home except for when his wife drove him a few miles to eat a sandwich lunch by the sea. He had been on dialysis for years. A kidney transplant was now out of the question. He did not complain, in fact he gave the impression that he had learned to live contentedly within the boundaries, no longer refusing to accept them. Although I do not think he would have called himself a religious man he gave thanks for each day. I felt I could learn something from him.

Earlier he and Ann had talked together. She would pray for him, I thought. Her twin brother, Peter, had died in his forties from kidney failure after prolonged dialysis, and a rejected kidney transplant.

That night, around 9 pm, he became critically ill. Chronic kidney failure. His curtains were drawn but no one in the ward slept. There was a constant coming and going, muted voices. It was decided to summon his relatives. They came soon after midnight. I fell asleep around 3 am and awoke at six o'clock when the ward stirred. As I opened my eyes I looked across the bay. The curtains had been drawn back, he was propped up in bed with pillows. His eyes were open. I waved. He waved back.

The Rev. Pat Pilditch from a Barnstaple Anglican church, whom I had met five years before at Lee Abbey, came towards my bed smiling in her long blue robes. Would I like a brief service of Holy Communion in the ward? I welcomed the privilege so Ruth delayed her departure to be present. She read the lesson.

'Draw near with faith, and take this holy sacrament to your comfort; and make your humble confession to Almighty God.' There was quiet in the ward. Pat did not speak the familiar words too loudly, so as not to intrude on others, but I sensed everyone was straining to listen, some perhaps remembering.

'The body of. . . . The blood of Christ preserve your body and soul into everlasting life.' She prayed for all in the bay, in the hospital, while gently laying hands on my head. I sent up a silent prayer for the patient who had been so ill in the night.

Ann saw Ruth off from the car park. It was an emotional parting. When she returned, Gordon, my brother, had arrived unannounced from Sheffield. On Sunday when he phoned the ward he told the nurse he had only just heard of my heart attack. 'You must be the very last person,' she said.

Now retired, after teaching law, he was working voluntarily three days a week in a local hospice, finding fulfilment in helping with accounts, assisting in the kitchen Saturday evenings, and driving terminally ill patients out for what was sometimes their final fling. 'Is there somewhere you'd specially like to go?' he'd ask. One lady mentioned a beauty spot in Derbyshire. Content when she had been there, she died in the car as he drove her back into the city.

'I wanted you to see me, Edward, with your own eyes,' he said, rosy cheeked and rather pleased with himself. 'I knew a glimpse of me would convince you that you couldn't be in heaven!'

As a young man, Gordon was a keen Christian, now he rarely went to church. His coming and his wit were a tonic. With a gift for telling stories, most of which we believed, he took our thoughts beyond Barnstaple and then escorted Ann out to a jolly lunch.

He had one complaint, 'I've come all this way and he looks so well.'

'An answer to prayer,' Ann said.

'No one prays for me,' he grinned. She told him we did.

That night I wanted to write Ann a letter of thanks for her love and support. I had no note paper, no energy. On a page torn from my diary I scrawled, 'I love you.' When I gave it to her she said she would keep it for ever.

'Cardiac arrest. Trinity ward. Cardiac arrest. Trinity.' Ann heard the frightening alert in the hospital foyer as she was on her way to the car. A doctor rushed past her, a bleep in his hand. Her heart beat rapidly. A patient on Trinity, in a critical condition. Cardiac arrest meant a loss of consciousness, absence of pulse. To minimise the risk of brain damage resuscitation starts at once. She knew that like all major hospitals this one had a cardiac arrest team ready. They would drop whatever they were doing to respond. The doctor racing towards the lift was part of it.

She did a turn around and slowly, deliberately made for Trinity herself, praying for the patient, praying so hard I was safe. 'Don't panic. He's not the only patient in Trinity.'

The lift doors closed slowly. It began its ascent. She recalled the red emergency button in the ward for such emergencies, the resuscitation equipment within reach, the experienced nurses who knew precisely what to do and would not waste a second. She walked from the lift, through the swing doors, along the corridor.

I was sitting up in bed fully conscious. I smiled at her. The cardiac patient was being wheeled from another bay into mine where additional resources were available. I could not tell if he was alive. One of the half-a-dozen staff crowded round the bed drew the curtains.

Thirty minutes or so later the patient, bed and all, were wheeled out. Was he being taken to intensive care? Had he died? We didn't think so. I caught a glimpse of him later in the week, fragile but very much in this world. It was good to know. Fellow patients were becoming family. Such dramas, part of normal hospital life, do not make the headlines but there was no doubt he owed his life to the rapid response of the standby team, the availability of the defibrillator.

Joy, joy. I was allowed to make my first visit to the toilet. The nurse took me there in a wheelchair. 'Don't lock the door.' She pointed to a buzzer. 'If you want you can try to walk back with me holding your arm.'

I had counted as other patients went. It was about fifteen or sixteen paces. When she returned I ducked it.

'I'll walk next time, nurse.' She was content to accept the promise.

By the following day I was able to walk around my bed unaided and to reach the toilet, staying close to the wall for support. No mountaineer could have had a bigger sense of achievement, but I had in addition a sense of thankfulness to God. What had the prophet written? 'For I am the Lord, your God, who takes hold of your right hand and says to you, "Do not fear; I will help you"' (Isaiah 41:13, NIV).

Excitement from the air came in the shape of a yellow air-sea rescue helicopter. Those who were mobile hurried to the window in their dressing gowns to see a patient being delivered. A medical team was waiting. A stretcher was whisked into casualty. One of our group, a local farmer, spoke with confidence: 'That's almost certainly a holiday-maker who was cut off by the tide, or who had a heart attack walking up Clovelly.'

Ann read Psalm 121 aloud and copied out a few verses to keep by me. 'I will lift my eyes to the hills – where does my help come from? My help cometh from the Lord, the maker of heaven and earth.' On another card she had written the promise, 'The Lord will keep you from all harm – he will watch over your life; the Lord will watch over your coming and going, both now and for evermore.'

She returned the next morning to find I had been moved to another bay in Trinity ward, where I was not under the watchful eye of the nurses twenty-four hours a day. I had a bed by the window where I could see the green hills.

'It's nearer the exit,' I pointed out to some community members from Lee Abbey who called in while shopping in Barnstaple. The early June sunshine warmed me and my spirits soared. The five other patients were congenial, some recovering from surgery, one about to be taken by ambulance to London for a coronary by-pass. I was able to have a shower, a chair being provided in it, then return to my bed for a rest before shaving. I surprised myself by feeling happy, optimistic about the future. I was not about to die.

I laughed at a card from two former Hodder colleagues, who were now the publishers of Monarch Books. 'Come off it, God,' Tony and Jane Collins had written, 'we still need this bloke. You can't have him yet.'

Ann wrote in her journal:

> This evening he was talking about my going home now and he could come by train – something upset him about arriving home – always so much to do – and he'd like me to be there. So I must think out what to do and ask people to sort things out as much as possible. I'm sure Jean would help – get bread, milk, eggs and such like for me. Glad I left it all fairly well organised. I think! Please give me wisdom. The emotion of cards, letters he can't deal with. The mental and emotional healing takes longer than the physical – grieving for the loss of a healthy body.
>
> As I came out of the ward tonight a thrush was singing. The rain had stopped and he was in the bush by the car-park steps singing his heart out – praising you I like to think. I've been feeling so much more normal today. Thank you, Lord.

The bed next to me had been empty for a couple of days until a rather tubby young man arrived. I said hello but he turned away. The staff obviously knew him well; he had been in before. He was well spoken and something made me think he had a privileged background. I tried again to make conversation without success. He obviously did not wish to establish contact and I respected his desire for privacy but was disturbed when I heard him sobbing.

Then, shortly before lights were dimmed for the night,

I witnessed a lovely act. A motherly orderly, who a little earlier had brought us an evening drink, returned and sat on his bed as he drank his cocoa. They talked quietly, her arm around him. When she left she tucked him up and kissed him on the cheek. He fell asleep, the cuddly toy in his arms. What remarkable care the National Health Service provides.

Ann was feeling the prolonged strain. She confided to her journal:

> Thank you for saving me from a bump as I was moving my car in the car park. The other driver probably thought I was moving out. Nearly had a bump yesterday, so please help me Lord.
>
> I've had to be without Edward to lean on at a very tough time – that's what seemed so bad the first day or two, when I'm used to discussing things with him – having to make my own decisions.
>
> I'm bound to feel all muddled and confused now, Lord, the anxiety, stress, tiredness – living has been muddled and confused – sorting out clothes, getting them washed, dried, trying to be as unobtrusive in the household as I can, feeling very thankful to them, and grateful for their taking me in so lovingly and kindly. It was impressive to hear them in the Bible study in their home last night – Elaine said lots of practical, helpful things.
>
> Ruth said I was a 'bag-lady' and I've felt a bit like that taking my bag every day, planning for the day, things in the car, all a jumble – the 'wrong' room in Lee Abbey was nothing to this.

She was encouraged, we both were, when her sister and husband George arrived from their isolated, hilltop home on Exmoor. George had retired after an army career and they had fallen in love with an old farmhouse with spellbinding views. If their generator was not working they used oil lamps; when the water supply behind their home was used up during a dry summer they walked down to the river with containers. The postman left the mail at a point about a mile away, and they made a weekly trip to the nearest village for supplies and a more infrequent visit to a supermarket in Minehead. And they were happy, blissfully so.

Ann shared with them her apprehension about the long journey home when she would have to do all the driving. I tried to conceal mine. I liked to be at the wheel, in control. In an emergency I would be useless. I could barely walk twenty yards. I couldn't lift a small bag. I had arrived at the hospital critically ill ten days before. I was leaving out of danger, in a positive frame of mind but with little strength, utterly dependent on Ann.

Dr George would see me on Saturday to decide if we could make the journey on Sunday when the traffic was lighter. At no point would we be more than sixty miles from a large hospital – Exeter, Southampton, Chichester, London. On her return journey Ruth had made a list of places where we could find refreshments and toilets, all within a few yards of parking. We studied it closely.

'Please doctor, I want to go home. And when will I be allowed to drive again?'

The sixth lesson is one that I would have to repeat to myself again and again in coming days:

Live within the limits.

The Sixth Lesson

LIVE WITHIN THE LIMITS

When you pass through the waters I will be with you; and through the rivers, they shall not overwhelm you; when you walk through fire you shall not be burned, and the flame shall not consume you.

—*Isaiah 43:2 (RSV)*

When trouble hits us we can react to it in a variety of ways. We can let it knock us out, so that we lose all hope and stamina. We can rebel and refuse to accept the rightness or merit of it. We can fill our lives with feverish activity so that we have no time to think about it. Or we can accept it – without defeat, rebellion or evasion – trusting that God will make clear tomorrow what is so difficult to understand today.

—*George Appleton,* Journey for a Soul

'What would happen if this were not done at all?' If the answer is, 'Nothing would happen,' then obviously the conclusion is to stop doing it. It is amazing how many things busy people are doing that will never be missed!

—*Peter Drucker,* The Effective Executive

Chapter Seven

A happy day looking forward to Edward's going home.
Steve was busy cutting hedges and mowing the lawn. Elaine
and I planted a wheelbarrow with geraniums and lobelia
after I got back from seeing Edward this evening. Please
help me with the driving tomorrow, Lord, help Edward
with being a passenger, keep us safe, may all go well. And
assist us in all the adjustment of the coming days to stay
close to you and close to one another.

Thank you for this home and family. Elaine said last night
they'd been praying together about the journey. This has
been a good week with them, happy times mixed up with it
all.

We thanked the hard-working staff who had served us
with such consideration, left a gift for the nurses, and
with Ann carrying my few belongings, made for the lift.
Each wobbly step – past the hospital shop selling newspapers, chocolates, greeting cards – took us nearer home,
the most desired destination. I sat on a bench by the exit
while Ann brought the car up to the door, the passenger
seat already in a semi-reclining position. I would be a less
troublesome passenger if I fell asleep; she thought so,
and I agreed.

I was elated as the car pulled away and remained that

way for several minutes until the car reached the centre of Barnstaple, one of the oldest towns in Britain. Apart from a milkman and a paperboy with the heavy Sunday newspapers the town was deserted, curtains still drawn. At our first roundabout my excitement was replaced by terror. I began to sweat.

'Can you slow down, Ann? Please. I'm frightened.'

'I haven't exceeded twenty yet, love. We've a long way to go.' Was I going to be like this all the way to Sussex?

'It's the buildings, the shops, the houses, they're all moving. I'm scared.' She glanced at me and reluctantly slowed to a crawl. For ten days nothing had progressed in my enclosed world at faster than walking speed. The patients who eventually made it to the bathroom were slow and hesitant, the visitors entered the wards diffidently and the nurses though purposeful gave the appearance of being unhurried. My eyes, my head, couldn't adjust to this bigger world. A couple of drivers overtook us impatiently. My demand to go slower was unsettling for Ann who was normally the passenger.

'Try closing your eyes until we're out of town. Then it's open country. No buildings to move. You'll be fine then.'

I closed my eyes knowing if I didn't I'd soon be asking to go back to the hospital and I didn't want that. A little later, sensing she was increasing speed, I looked around to see green fields on both sides of the road, a cluster of hills in the distance, clear blue skies above. Panic passed as I soaked in the warmth of the sun, noted the well-surfaced road and the absence of other vehicles. I watched out for signposts, noting how many miles we had covered. At a steady fifty to sixty we were making considerable headway.

'With no hold-ups we'll be home by teatime,' I

declared happily. By mid-day we had reached the M3 motorway, pulling into the service station for a light lunch. I couldn't walk more than fifty yards or so but we were able to park close to the main entrance. Ann fetched the food while I sat contentedly at the table by the entrance eyeing the sausages, eggs and chips, or roast beef and Yorkshire pudding which were the popular choices on other tables. Ann brought tuna sandwiches and I didn't complain.

The temperature soared that afternoon and the belt around my waist began to melt as the sun streamed in, leaving a permanent black mark on my trousers and the shirt underneath. We said a prayer as we reached the crowded M25, the most scary motorway in Britain.

'You're a fine driver, Ann,' I said after covering 200 miles. Apparently I had never complimented her on her driving before.

'Please repeat that. I want to hear it again. Perhaps I could have it in writing.'

'No one could have driven better than you've done,' I said, temporarily relinquishing my normal male arrogance.

'Friends have been praying,' she said modestly, adding, 'and next time I have a car I'd like an automatic.'

'Look, it's still there,' I said as we saw our house and pulled into the driveway. 'What a glorious, beautiful sight.'

There was a bowl of flowers in the hall, a tray set for tea in the dining room; in the fridge were ham, eggs and milk. There was a message and a bowl of fruit from Rosemary and Peter Scott, our housegroup leaders, while our friend Jean had made a sponge cake. Our good neighbours Eric and Joan had made our key available to them. A bed in a ground-floor room was made up and waiting. Wearily, blithely, I collapsed into it.

'I never knew I loved home so greatly. It's wonderful to be here. So restful, so peaceful, so quiet.' I looked around the simply furnished bedroom. 'And it's so beautiful.'

Ann was overwhelmed by the thoughtfulness of neighbours, and our friends in the church and the office. Ten days ago she thought she might be returning home alone. That night while I slept downstairs she wrote:

> How heavenly to be in my own bed in our lovely quiet home, feeling as if it's just welcoming us, and putting its arms around us. I just caught sight of the title of Julian of Norwich's *Enfolded in Love* and was looking something up in my old journal and read: 'I have covered you with the shadow of my hand.'
>
> A long day – eight-year-old Sophie sitting next to me at the breakfast bar asked: 'Do you want to go?'
>
> 'I'm glad to be going home but am sorry to be leaving you.' In the past few days this family has become very dear.

We both slept like children and the next day I surprised myself and Ann by climbing the stairs to our first-floor lounge without difficulty. From an easy chair I looked at the wide view over Ashdown Forest with the North Downs in the distance. Our oak was in full leaf, the pines gently swaying, blue smoke ascending from a garden bonfire in the valley, the Hartfield church spire clearly visible across the valley. A tree creeper scooted up the wind-bent larch and a squirrel warily crossed the sloping lawn watching out for Zac, our Burmese cat. His full name was Zacchaeus so named because as a kitten he was forever climbing trees when he was not scrambling through a neighbour's window or onto the garage roof.

Here was an oasis of peace, the ideal spot in which to bid farewell to the drivenness, the urgency which had dominated my life. A place for reading books, for music and gazing at sunsets; for learning to question priorities, to accept when I'd done enough, to be realistic about achievement.

I recalled editing an article for *Renewal* by Eric Bird on the myth of the spiritual superman. He was talking chiefly of the need for shared leadership in the church.

How many ministers are struggling, burned out, depressed, over-tired, neglecting their families, pressurised and overworked, primarily because they are labouring under the false expectation that they have to be superman he asked. The spiritual superman is a myth – just like the film *Superman*. If we will stop believing the legend we will do ourselves, our families and our churches a great favour.

Had I been attempting to be superman? My close friends never thought of me as such, and seeing my stumbling efforts would laugh at the suggestion, but in my pride had I been behaving like that? Attempting the impossible and failing to rise above the mediocre?

I reached for a favoured biography *Dr Sangster* written by his son Paul. After his death I had been privileged to act for a time as the literary agent for the great Methodist preacher who Sunday after Sunday filled London's Westminster Central Hall with 2,500 people. 'The only thing my father never found time for was rest,' Paul wrote. 'The fever for work never left him.'

In 1958, the year he died, still in his fifties, Dr Sangster wrote: 'All my life I have been full of energy, zest, enthusiasm, gaiety, bright conversation, quick repartee. But now I am prematurely aged, tired with a tiredness sleep cannot cure, slurred in my speech and unable to walk.' Among his papers marked *Quite Private* Paul found these words written at the time. 'I rushed about too much. I talked too much. I didn't pray enough. I was proud of my health and work. The trouble was in the will – I lashed my body on, imprisoned in a timetable.' Paul wrote how his father came to regret his fever for work.

After lunch I returned to bed and slept until wakened by the telephone in the hall. Ann answered it. 'He's doing marvellously, thank you. Yes, the journey was great. Edward said it was as if the angels had transported us home. Well, I was at the wheel but they certainly accompanied us.'

The caller offered to visit us. I heard Ann hesitate. I had placed her in an impossible situation. 'It's so kind of you, and we'd really love to see you both, but he's asked not to have visitors this week. Says he needs time to adjust. I hope you'll understand.'

They said they did and probably didn't. Neither did Ann. I was being selfish, but felt I couldn't cope emotionally with the sympathy, the kindness, the questions. I wanted to be sheltered from having to make a response. Visitors would talk about what had happened at Lee Abbey, in Barnstaple, and I didn't want that however well intentioned. I was disregarding Ann's understandable need for people, for someone to share with. I didn't even want our greatly appreciated vicar yet.

Ann confided to her journal:

I feel sad about Andrew. Don't let him feel rejected. But I have to let Edward decide. It was lovely to be relaxed and potter around the shops in Crowborough, though driving my car was a bit of a come down after Edward's – noisy, hard to steer. Everyone seemed in a hurry – they must be more amiable and slower in Barnstaple and going to the lift in Waitrose reminded me of the hospital lift. Dear Reggie and Joan were coming but I suggested they wait as I thought that was what Edward would want. I didn't feel anxious about leaving him. He didn't feel anxious about being left. We both want to get back to normal. He feels he has more

88

years yet, maybe different. I feel one day I will have to face losing him.

Ian came with flowers, two beautiful hibiscus from the church. Prue brought a lovely tub of flowers. So much love and kindness.

Ann blossomed when she met people. I appreciated them equally but sometimes felt drained afterwards. Friends were part of her nourishment and she hated to miss the opportunity of meeting but nobly didn't complain. On Tuesday, she called at the vicarage. Andrew was out. Katherine prayed and chatted with her.

We relaxed together in the colourful garden chairs and divided up *The Times*, Ann doing the crossword while I dozed off. After a mug of tea I walked the few yards down to our tiny pond to feed the four goldfish which the heron had left for another day, then out of breath stumbled back up the slight incline sinking breathlessly into the chair. After a rest I walked round the outside of the house, wondering how soon before I could walk up the hill, past our neighbour's house, to the small red postbox on the corner.

'Measure your progress by the lampposts,' someone advised. As we had no lampposts in the road I substituted trees, most days reaching another one. Our ageing West Highland terrier accompanied me and was surprised at my new tolerance when she stopped to sniff.

Our GP, Dr Sampson, called and confirmed the low-fat diet and advised no heavy lifting. I must not consider returning to the office for some weeks but he didn't say I couldn't phone. I was careful not to ask. Ann permitted one brief phone call to my secretary, Carol Lewry, every day, with a maximum of three or four minutes. Carol played along, asking just one question and selecting an easy one from her list. The more complicated matters could wait, or be dealt with in consultation with other senior staff: Wallace Boulton, Jane Bromham and Penny Thomas. Every day there were encouragements, although progress could not be hastened. Ann drove me to the cafe on Ashdown Forest, two or three miles from home, for a pot of tea. We sat outside sheltered by a sunshade and life seemed idyllic. After a week she took me to Eastbourne, twenty-three miles distant, so we could sit and gaze at the sea.

'It's wonderful to be able to rejoice in good things,' she wrote in her journal. 'To be peaceful, able to sleep, in good spirits, helped by the next bit of progress.'

Our friend, Dr Maxwell Jones, phoned from London, to remind us how thirteen years before he had suffered an almost fatal heart attack. Now seventy-eight he was still doing regular locums. His call was a confidence booster and yet after the euphoria of being home I found myself becoming increasingly afraid of the future. It was not death I feared but life.

It probably started with the arrival of the bank statement. I always checked it on the calculator, a simple enough task taking a few minutes. Now after two hours of trying I gave up, making an unsuccessful second attempt the following day, but my mind was not functioning as it should. Was this temporary or permanent? It was tough enough being physically feeble without the mind being affected. I was too frightened to mention it even to Ann. I told myself I didn't want to worry her but that was only part of the truth. I should have known that anxieties are best talked about, brought into the open, that we need someone to help us admit and face them. I buried mine deep.

I welcomed Ann's proposal of a game of Scrabble later that week. We had been evenly balanced as players – well, maybe she got the top score slightly more often –for while I made quick, almost instant moves, she pondered long. Now I lost by a wide margin. We played again, her score higher, mine even lower. And so it continued.

'You're a good loser,' she said, meaning it as a compliment.

'I'm having a lot of practice.'

I sat at the portable, electronic typewriter to send a thank-you letter to Carol and everyone at the office but after two or three attempts I gave up. My fingers were repeatedly hitting the wrong keys. I became tense thinking about it, wakeful during the night, puzzled that no one had mentioned this as a possible outcome of a heart attack.

With the Palmist I wanted to cry:

> Save me, O God!
> For the waters have come up to my neck.
> I sink in deep mire,
>   where there is no foothold;
> I have come into deep waters,
>   and the flood sweeps over me.
>
> (Psalm 69:1,2, RSV)

It was less demanding, less frightening for me to look to books rather than people and there were plenty in our home. I turned again to Paul Tournier, the Swiss counsellor and author for whom I had been privileged to publish – although SCM were his main publisher in Britain. In *Creative Suffering* he suggested that suffering, of whatever kind, was the real test of a person. 'What is our personal attitude to life and its changes and chances?' he asked, proposing that a positive, creative reaction developed the person, while a negative one stunted him. While some of his patients transformed misfortunes creatively, others went under. 'A man's value is to be measured not so much by his successes, as by the way he takes his failure,' was a maxim he quoted.

He acknowledged that genuine acceptance takes time, passing through various stages, from refusal, through anger and revolt, and that it is not helpful to pretend, to force, premature acceptance. To be able to say 'yes' without hesitation, in the midst of misfortune, was a gift of grace. Could I say 'yes' to the future, believing all my tomorrows were in God's hands? To incapacity, whether mental or physical, to any misfortune? I thought again of my father's final year after his cruel stroke. 'Not that, Lord, not that.' I prayed. The best I could hope for was that whatever the situation, at the appropriate moment, I would be given that gift of grace Dr Tournier wrote about.

Three weeks after returning home I attended early communion at All Saints. This was the smallest of the three morning services with about forty in attendance and I walked without faltering from the pew to the altar rail to receive the bread and the wine. It was a holy occasion and one of quiet thanksgiving. Watching others go forward, after I returned to my seat, I saw friends who had faced misfortune, especially bereavement, who had eventually reached the state of acceptance. Now they were positive, creative people reaching out to others in their troubles.

Partly concealed from me, the emotion and uncertainty of life was beginning to catch up with Ann. She wrote in her journal:

Tonight I am not so unafraid. In fact I am afraid, Lord, of losing Edward, of being alone. With his steady improvement I'm forgetting the seriousness of what happened – yet we need to move on, to be able to enjoy what you give us.

He's had some chest pain, quickly relieved by GTN tablets. It's the first time he has had angina, and didn't say until I asked – he's done a lot today – gone to the office for half an hour. We went to the forest and sat relaxed in the car. Then, at another car park, we sat for ages, and it was peaceful and beautiful in the sunshine.

Lord, you kept him safe that Saturday on the Downs when he was up there alone – you cared for him at Lee Abbey, in every way you provided help. Hold him in your arms tonight and enable me to know you are at my right hand; you are enfolding me with your love. Please help me to experience this tonight.

On the forest, Ann accompanying me, I learned to walk more normally again along the relatively flat well-marked paths, distances gradually lengthening. After-wards we would go to the forest cafe for tea. Such simple pleasures provided moments of contentment, of relaxa-tion with each other, of observing the natural world, the heather coming into bloom. And we kept an open eye for Winnie-the-Pooh for it was here, in this forest, that he would tiptoe, having those magic adventures which still draw visitors from around the world. One afternoon at Pooh Bridge everyone else was from Japan.

In Winnie-the-Pooh territory my seventh lesson began to impress itself on me:

Appreciate today.

APPRECIATE TODAY

The present moment holds infinite riches beyond your wildest dreams but you will only enjoy them to the extent of your faith and love. The more a soul loves, the more it longs, the more it hopes, the more it finds. The will of God is manifest in each moment, an immense ocean which the heart only fathoms in so far as it overflows with faith, trust and love.

—*Jean-Pierre de Caussade*

Admiral Byrd left a detailed record of manning an advanced weather base in Antarctic in the Winter of 1934. One day he almost died after being poisoned by fumes from a faulty stove. He wrote, 'I did take away something that I had not fully appreciated before; appreciation of the sheer beauty and miracle of being alive.'

Kilvert's Diary by the Rev. Francis Kilvert, demonstrates the joy which comes from an appreciation of the present moment.

> As I came down the hill into the valley across the golden meadows and along the flower-scented hedges a great wave of emotion and happiness stirred and rose up within me. I know not why I was so happy, nor what I was expecting, but I was in a delirium of joy, it was one of the supreme moments of existence, a deep delicious draught from the strong sweet cup of life. It came unsought, unbidden, at the meadow stile, it was one of the flowers of happiness scattered for us and found unexpectedly by the way of life.

Chapter Eight

Our diaries said we should be on *Queen Elizabeth 2* heading across the Atlantic for New York where, attracted by a massive price reduction, we had planned to spend three nights before flying home. I had never been on a large ocean liner although Ann had commenced her missionary life with a sea journey to Singapore. It was cheaper then than going by air. On receipt of a doctor's certificate the travel agency refunded our deposit almost in full. If we took a holiday it would be nearer home without the humidity of Manhatten. I knew from summer business trips how unpleasant it could be sandwiched between the skyscrapers, restless humanity crowding the pavements, yellow-cab drivers frustrated and impatient. One needed to be one hundred per cent fit to appreciate what Bernard Levin called its 'perpetual restlessness, its implacable determination never to keep still long enough to be defined'. The buildings one remembers have been knocked down and rebuilt, then replaced again. Most publishers have left for healthier, cheaper locations but numerous tempting bookshops remain.

On a Monday morning well into my recovery I had a light breakfast and showered. Troubled with angina I returned to bed instead of dressing. Two, three tiny white GTN tablets placed under the tongue, which normally brought swift relief, had no effect. A throbbing, like a heavy hammer, enveloped my back and chest and rapidly became more severe. I began to sweat.

Keep calm, I told myself, no need to be anxious. Anxiety could add to this problem. Lie still, think positively, breathe naturally. Sunday had been a quiet happy day and we had attended both morning and evening services. Having a problem like this at home wasn't like being alone on the South Downs or away from home in Lee Abbey. Ann was on the phone, I could hear her, but she'd come at once if I called.

Christie, our white West Highland terrier, peeped round the door and warily entered the bedroom which was normally out of bounds. She limply wagged her tail. Why wasn't I dressed? What sort of a master was I? The sun was shining, so I couldn't blame the weather. At this hour she didn't like to let me out of her sight in case I slipped out without her. She had quickly become accustomed to my presence during the day.

The hammer blows intensified, and a cramping tightness. I heard the phone being replaced.

'Ann, can you come please? I can't breathe.'

'What's wrong, love?'

'I've got a problem. My heartbeat's gone crazy. Can you find the window key? I need fresh air.'

Outwardly the complete professional, she took my wrist, felt my pulse, asked me to describe the symptoms.

'I'll get the doctor. He'll be in surgery now. I'll explain it's an emergency.'

A fresh-faced capable young doctor, new to the group practice, responded promptly, taking out his stethoscope, checking my blood pressure, saying little. He dialled for an ambulance as I gasped for breath, then gave an injection. We were fortunate. The ambulance station, like the surgery, was only minutes away. God be praised for the National Health Service.

Again I was impressed, had reason to be grateful, to the paramedics. I remember little of the swaying twenty-minute journey to the Kent and Sussex Hospital in Tunbridge Wells. Ann came in the ambulance, strapped in, unable to hold my hand, praying furiously as she watched the heart rate careering upwards, wondering if I would survive.

This was the hospital where seventeen years before I had gone to identify Gwen before the post mortem from which I learned she had lung cancer. During the previous week her GP, not in Crowborough, had been prescribing cough mixture for her cough and breathing difficulties. The possibility of cancer had not been mentioned. He was as shocked as I was. The memory came dully to mind as, attached to the now familiar high-tech monitoring equipment, I was whisked through the emergency entrance.

A cluster of doctors and nurses awaited our arrival. Another injection, an oxygen mask, a swift examination. Outside the doors a paramedic put a fatherly arm around Ann's shoulder, and a nurse produced a cup of tea.

'Lord, if I die, please look after Ann.'

It was five weeks since the heart attack. This problem was linked but different, more to do with the heart rate than blocked arteries. Equally threatening, if it couldn't be checked, but with less pain.

Ann telephoned our friends, Paul and Marian Bishop, two of the leaders on the pastoral staff of All Saints and St Richard's. Warm-hearted, sympathetic, perfect companions in an emergency, they detected the anxiety in her voice as well as in what she said. 'We'll come at once,' they said, dropping their schedule for the rest of the day.

The medication was taking effect. My pulse had slowed. An hour passed.

'We're taking your husband to intensive care,' the doctor told Ann. She sat in the waiting room appreciating the solace of Marian and Paul's presence, wondering what was happening, then becoming alarmed as the wait was prolonged. Had they forgotten her? She pressed the bell to ask the nurse if she could see me.

'Sorry, I'm afraid you'll have to wait a little longer.'

Fresh problems had developed. As I was sitting up to be examined my heart rate had again soared dangerously. For almost an hour the medical staff gathered round but I was barely aware of them. It was a more severe recurrence of what had happened earlier. Well, I was now in hospital and not waiting for an ambulance.

'Lord, please care for Ann.'

Where was she? Eventually, I was aware of her soothing presence. She sat with me for a while as the medical staff drifted away. We said little, neither of us feeling like talking, simply glad to be together for a few minutes, coming to terms with what was happening in our own ways.

Should she slip home to attend to the dog, get my pyjamas and toilet things? She found it difficult to think clearly, and turned to Paul and Marian outside, for advice.

'Well it won't take long,' Paul said. 'And you can return in your own car.'

'But suppose he needs me. I'd hate not to be here. And I need to decide about my evening clinic.' She was silent, trying to think things through. 'Let's go,' she said finally.

That morning she had read *Living Light*: 'Don't be bewildered or surprised when you go through fiery trials. Instead be really glad – because these trials will make you partners with Christ in his suffering and afterwards you will have the wonderful joy of sharing his glory in that coming day when it is to be displayed.'

She fed the dog and let her run round the garden for two or three minutes while she collected various items, then hurried back hardly daring to think how I might be. This was her fiery trial. The morning reading had gone on to speak of the comfort and hope which Christ gives and she reached out for them. She hurried along the endless corridors and pressed the bell outside intensive care and the nurse said I was well enough to see her. She gasped with relief.

Later Andrew our vicar arrived, in a red bow tie, pleated white shirt, grey suit. On his day off he was going to the opera in London. His dashing outfit cheered me.

'I wish you'd dress like this one Sunday!'

Meanwhile, the consultant talked privately with Ann outside the unit. He knew she was a doctor.

A supraventricular tachycardia, he said. More investigations. Probably an angiogram. For the intermittent heaviness in my right leg he would prescribe warfarin, for my heart verapamil. By late evening the heart-beat was stable, the drama over and Ann felt able to leave me.

Helen, from the office, kept Ann company at home that night. She was a caring person as well as a gifted artist whose paintings were sought after. One of them hung in our hall.

'I hope you won't be disturbed in the night,' Ann said. 'I'll keep my clothes ready in case there's an emergency.' Shortly before eleven she turned to her journal:

It all seemed to happen so quickly and I got so frightened – we've been feeling life is getting back to normal, he's been getting more energy.

Somehow it's different this time though some things are the same – waiting alone, Edward separated from me by illness and pain, finding my way around another strange hospital, phones etc, trying to think – not functioning very well at all – wondering however I could cope without him, appreciating being able to wash him, care for him, hanging on to you Lord, your promise to be at my right hand. . . . Oh, Lord, please watch over him tonight, give him peaceful, healing sleep.

The entry went on longer than usual, reliving the events of the day, and concluding, 'It's good to be in my own bed this time.'

I slept a little after the nurse had kindly moved my bed away from a distressed man who was crying in pain. When visitors arrived for him before dawn I knew his condition was critical. His bed was empty in the morning.

No one had to tell me that I had again been in the courtyard of heaven. In recent weeks I had thought a lot about going there. Once David Winter, later to become Head of BBC Religious Broadcasting, had introduced me at a booksellers' lunch where I was the speaker. 'When Edward arrives at the gates of heaven,' he said, 'he will forget to ask the Apostle Peter whether his name is in the Book of Life. Instead he'll ask who published it!'

In my study I had a copy of *Heaven, Better By Far* by J. Oswald Sanders. He had written it when he was ninety because so little about heaven was ever mentioned in the pulpit. He had been overwhelmed, as he wrote the book, by the magnitude and splendour of God's plan for the future. His own anticipation had been quickened and deepened. Shortly after finishing the manuscript he died.

Sanders started chapter one with Paul's words in Philippians 1:21–23 – 'For me, to live is Christ and to die is gain. If I am to go on living in the body, this will mean fruitful labour for me. Yet what shall I choose? I do not know! I am torn between the two: I desire to depart and be with Christ, which is far better.' He quoted Wolfgang Mozart, who died when he was thirty-five: 'I never go to bed without reflecting on the thought that perhaps, young as I am, the next day I might not be alive any more. And no man who knows me will be able to say that in social intercourse I am morose or sad.' In recent days I had watched the dawn break with a sense of gratitude for the gift of another day. This morning was no exception as light came gradually through the window behind my bed.

Was Ann awake too? I was sad for the suffering I had caused her in recent weeks, the uncertainty she now lived with, which this episode re-enforced. What a gift from God she was! More precious than gold. And a superb cook!

I was transferred to ward eight. It was due to be redecorated, the refurbishment long overdue. It was a Florence Nightingale ward, long lines of beds, too close together, overworked staff with constant journeys to and fro. A century away from the modern hospital in Barnstaple with its small bays surrounded by green hills. Here I saw with dismay paint peeling off the walls and watched with growing admiration the dedicated staff. I would support any claim for better pay, fewer hours, smaller wards.

An ex-professional footballer in the next bed was admitted during the night with agonising angina. He had played for a second or third division and now in his middle years was living alone in semi-poverty. The cheers from the terraces had become a memory, the goals were no longer being scored. He talked wistfully of the past.

He had no visitors. Like most others, I was not short of them, mostly from All Saints or my office. Some prayed with me, some simply sat, others made it easy for me to talk. Each was welcome. One afternoon three clergy came and said a prayer. Afterwards a patient wryly but not unkindly commented, 'If you don't get better swiftly now I'll lose my faith in the church.'

I sighed with relief when my housegroup leader and his wife, Peter and Rosemary, didn't pray, didn't move in with the full artillery.

To my surprise and relief I did not seem to have suffered any lasting consequences from this latest drama. I was promised a stress test on the treadmill, routine after a heart attack, an out-patient appointment which, including recovery time, would take about one hour. After that we could go on a holiday, somewhere close to home and a hospital.

My watch stopped. It worried me. I couldn't see a clock and I liked to know the time. As an expression of confidence in the future, Ann bought me a Swiss replacement, the best and most expensive watch I'd ever owned. 'A bit pricey this,' I said, proudly strapping it to my wrist. I held my arm out above the bedclothes to admire it. It was sufficiently clear to see in the half-light of the ward during the hours of darkness.

'I wanted the best,' she smiled. 'It has to last you a long time. Like years.' We looked at each other.

'I'll treasure it – for years.'

It was the most thoughtful and meaningful present, sending all the correct messages. When she left my eyes kept returning to it, as a young woman's might to her engagement ring. Without a watch I was like a blind man who has mislaid his white stick. I recalled my first watch which my grandmother had presented to me on my fifth birthday, a year after my mother died, leaving three sons, of whom I was the eldest. Norman was a few days old.

Before our engagement, my first gift to Ann had been a watch, but not as fine a one as this. I told the jeweller it must have a second hand (essential for taking the pulse of patients). But why a watch? It was probably an expression of my emphasis on time and punctuality. Better be twenty minutes early than two minutes late for a train, a church service, any appointment. My father had drilled it into us as children. Ann had a different perception. On one of our first dates she was almost two hours late. She had been in the operating theatre when a routine operation turned into a major one. She could hardly help that but there were occasions when it led to tension. A matter of temperament. We each had to learn from one another. And didn't.

I had read about the consultant who was told by his secretary that the chair seats in the reception area of the private clinic needed replacing. 'Only the fronts of the seats are worn,' she said. The cardiac specialist was not surprised. The well-to-do patients he was seeing were mostly business people who lived life on the edge of their chairs, a tempest blowing through their days.

Our church had a congregation which largely worshipped on the edge of their pews. With three Sunday morning services and more than 100 (yes, 100) small active groups and ministries we expanded while many parishes saw declining congregations. I told the vicar about a restaurant outside Bangkok where Ann and I had been guests. In the open air it covered several pleasant, well-watered acres so, to facilitate service, the waiters and waitresses were on roller-skates. They arrived to take our orders at a threatening speed and returned with equal haste with the hot dishes – without spillage. We remembered nothing of the food but will never forget the delivery.

'Andrew, All Saints is a church on roller-skates!' I announced over a cup of coffee together. Unlike some clergy he is not threatened by such comments. His hoot of laughter caused everyone to turn. Well, it's better to be a church on skates than on crutches.

It may be satisfying, it may be fun but is there a price to be paid for living life like this? Does it hint at an unbalanced emphasis on activity while neglecting the interior life? When Jesus commissioned his disciples to evangelise the world, was constant movement, that 'perpetual restlessness' which I love, what he had in mind?

During Lent a wise preacher had reminded us of Christ's question to Peter. 'Do you love me?' Not, do you serve me. 'Do you love me?' Not, are you constantly busy. I had no right to point the finger at anyone. I needed to reassess both in my public world and my private one what it meant to love and serve Christ. My eighth lesson, in the words of Mahatma Gandi, was:

There is more to life than increasing its speed.

The Eighth Lesson

THERE IS MORE TO LIFE THAN INCREASING ITS SPEED

More programmes, more meetings, more learning experiences, more relationships, more busyness, until one becomes so heavy at the surface of life that the whole person trembles on the verge of collapse. Fatigue, disillusionment, failure, defeat, all becoming frightening possibilities. The neglected private world can no longer hold the weight.

— *Gordon MacDonald,* Ordering Your Private World

Lord, you put twenty-four hours in a day, and gave me a body which gets tired and can only do so much. Show me the tasks you want me to do.

— *Angela Ashwin*

Chapter Nine

Being able to walk more than a mile without being faint or groggy – one foot behind the other, arms swinging gently, breathing deeply – was a surprisingly exhilarating tonic. Regular exercise, except on hot or icy days, was a prescribed medicine to be taken at least once daily. Our home was in an area with little traffic, with glimpses of well-tended lawns through beech or laurel hedges, summer flower beds, colourful garden furniture, so different from my boyhood home in Sheffield, where there were more pubs than trees.

I gradually became known to the dog walkers, largely mature women with smaller breeds. I shrugged if they overtook me, believing that it was temporary. The bigger dogs were exercised by their masters earlier in the day. I had the worthy intention of saying a simple prayer of blessing for every person I passed and did for a few days, then forgot. Please God, record my intentions and not my actions; they are usually worthier.

My week in intensive care and ward eight set me back a few notches, then the doctor gave the all clear I had been patiently anticipating since my return from Barnstaple. I could drive again. With Ann reinstalled in the passenger seat I took the car into Tunbridge Wells to the newly built Victoria Place shopping centre. There were seats along the arcades of shops and modestly priced restaurants where we could have a cup of tea or decaffeinated coffee and choose from a selection of newspapers. I pulled carefully into the adjacent multi-storey car park, my heart racing a little as I looked for an empty space. Ascending in the lift to Fenwicks on the seventh floor, Ann joined the short queue while I sat down and read one of the tabloids we would never dream of buying. When, after less than an hour, we returned to the car, content with our outing, there was a not-to-be-missed parking ticket on the windscreen. Concerned with parking, with making Fenwicks without mishap, I had overlooked to buy a ticket.

'Well, £20 is rather a lot to pay for coffee,' Ann said, but we paid without protest not wanting to spoil the day. In a sense it had been worth it.

I started to go to the Crowborough offices for two hours each morning. My colleagues had been calling at home but being separated from office life troubled me. I hungered for the daily routine, the unexpected chal-lenges, the little crises, the small triumphs. I missed the books, the magazines, the authors who wrote or phoned, a few famous, others barely known, most seeking encouragement. Several had dedicated their books to me. But most of all I missed those I worked with. Each had contributed to our steady growth. I had watched their children go from school to university, to find jobs, set up homes of their own. They were an extension of my family and like all relationships these had assumed a fresh import in my life. Was anything more primary? 'Life is only for love,' someone wrote. 'Time is only that we may find God.'

In his recent autobiography *Just as I Am*, Dr Billy Graham said he had many regrets looking back over his life and, in a far less significant existence, I share some of them. He admits he has failed many times, and there are things he would do differently.

> I would spend more time with my family. When I look back over the schedule I kept thirty or forty years ago, I am staggered by all the things we did and the engagements we kept. Sometimes we flitted from one part of the country to another, even from continent to continent, in the course of only a few days. Were all those engagements necessary? Was I as discerning as I might have been about which ones to take and which to turn down? I doubt it. Every day I was absent from my family is gone for ever. Although much of that travel was necessary, some of it was not.

I had given greater priority to work, especially to books, than to people. As my friend Rob Parsons said, 'Most of us spend our lives trying to please others because we need to be needed. Unfortunately we end up saying "no" to those who are dearest to us.'

'Go home, your job is wrecking you,' was a headline in *The Times*. I guess I was rediscovering that in the words of the well-worn cliché, 'people matter more than things'. Some of those people were family who, apart from dear Ann, lived miles away, others were in All Saints, and there were these colleagues in my office. Special, lovely people.

On my first morning back for a 9.30 am to 11.30 am spell, before I had permission to drive, Jane Bromham the production manager, collected me in her car and carried my almost empty briefcase into the office. She saw that lifting it was a strain as lifting anything was. It was humiliating but she was kindly, matter-of-fact, and passed no comment. Others seeing I remained a little unsteady on my feet when standing still, immediately pushed forward a chair when I entered their office, sheltered me from certain phone calls, concealed a few letters. It was a transient situation and there were daily indications of returning strength. I had pushed aside any foolish notion of retirement for five years, seeking the quiet satisfactions of office life, the opportunities for creativity, as others sought the companionship of a golf club or a pub.

I would take the stress test in my stride, a small hurdle to be cleared without difficulty, a marker on the path to a conventional working day. It would only last eight to ten minutes, the ECG registering any abnormality. Ann insisted on accompanying me to Kent and Sussex. I objected. 'I don't want to be nannied. I'm a man. I can drive the few miles there.' She came.

Inevitably arriving too early, while I waited I persuaded her to go and do some shopping she had mentioned. She'd be back in plenty of time to collect me; the doctor hadn't arrived and there was an eighty-year-old waiting before me. We'd been in ward eight together and he proudly told me he had mowed his lawn that weekend. He looked completely fit, his eyes bright in his cheery sun-tanned face.

'I still manage my own business,' he said, like a man after my own heart. 'And I'm going to sail through this,' he boasted. His relaxed appearance when he reappeared after twenty minutes added to my confidence and confirmed his optimism had been justified.

'Nothing to it,' he whispered. 'I did almost ten minutes. You start off at a crawl, then every couple of minutes they increase the pace; a bit of a challenge after six minutes but they switch off if it gets too much.' He straightened his tie, checked his jacket. 'A finger hovers over the stop button as they watch you and the monitor. Good luck.'

'Mr Edward England.'

A pleasing feminine voice, a tall woman in a white

coat. I followed her through the door. 'You can leave your jacket and shirt on the couch. Keep on your trousers and shoes. Come through when you're ready.'

I stood gingerly on the treadmill, electrodes on my chest, holding both handrails, while a young doctor casually examined my medical notes, a mug of tea by his side. Together they would monitor my progress. If the eighty-year-old managed I certainly could, and for two minutes had no problem. Easier than walking up our own road.

'We're going to increase the speed a little,' I was told. 'We'll switch it off if it proves too fast.' I smiled confidently.

I survived a matter of seconds, was assisted to a chair, then to the couch, struggling for breath, in obvious distress. I heard the doctor making a hurried phone call. In moments I was being wheeled into the ward with the peeling paint, relieved the triumphant eighty-year-old had gone.

Ann wrote:

I got to the clinic, looking for Edward, expecting him to be sitting waiting and was met by a young doctor who said, 'Mrs England?' He developed an arrhythmia on the stress test – hadn't gone long. In ward eight again. He was cold and shivery and no one had thought to cover him up. His chest was bare except for the ECG stickers. I fetched him another blanket. They were probably good medically but were not looking at him as a person, cold and ill. He did improve fairly quickly as he got oxygen and warmed up.

The doctor had about five stabs for a drip. SN Mary Cain was on duty so at least a familiar face – she was so kind, reassuring, said she'd seen many come in after a stress test.

Lord, it's been a feeling of 'snakes and ladders', or perhaps more accurately of walking up a sand dune then slipping back.

I was a miserable patient, discouraged, too well to be in hospital, yet unfit to pull my weight. I added to Ann's agony.

> He was fed up with being in hospital, angry with all sorts of things, telling me I was not a good conversationalist – I was so tired and with a sore throat and just wanted to go to bed and sleep. I couldn't seem to sum up any interesting conversation; though it was better after I'd been to the shopping precinct and had coffee and chocolate cake!
>
> I feel flattened but yesterday it was lovely to go to Marion and Don's (members of our church) for an evening meal and enjoy chatting with them. Thank you for them Lord, and for John Hobbs, Rosemary Scott, Val, Carol and Andrew.

I was home after five days. The angiogram in London was now a priority appointment. It came and went without mishap. A small catheter, under local anaesthetic, was inserted into the groin. The quietly spoken consultant said I could watch on a screen the tip of the catheter as it moved into each of the main arteries, visible because of the injection of a substance opaque to the X-rays. I saw my name appear on the screen but felt cheated when half an hour later I found myself being wheeled back into the lift to return to my room without having seen anything; asleep through it all.

'You'll be pleased it's over,' the nurse said brightly. 'Everything went well. You'll be staying in overnight, but can go home in the morning.'

The consultant came and sat on my bed, drew a picture of the heart and its arteries, explaining precisely what they had done. 'For the present we're going to rely on medication. If the angina persists we'll bring you back for angioplasty. I'll write to your GP.'

Ann stayed overnight in a London hotel, leaving her phone number with the staff nurse. 'I feel as if a great load has gone in that I was preparing myself for the worst – now I can look to the future for us. Please help me to learn from all this to keep priorities right, keep things in proportion, keep values right, keep relationships right.'

We celebrated by booking five days in the Swan Hotel, Southwold, in East Anglia, a few hours from home. Ann would share the driving. We lingered over the journey, making it part of the break.

Southwold turned out to be a glorious choice, a small elegant town, hardly changed in 500 years. Our bedroom overlooked the open-air market, where a few modest stalls were erected each morning before breakfast. There was a glimpse of the sea down the road. The other guests were older, quiet, reserved, very middle class. In the mornings we sauntered along the front, admired the famous greens; watched families with buckets and spades building castles, relaxing in deckchairs, making pots of tea in beach huts; the bravest ones bathing in the sea. We drove across heathlands, past impressive churches with few households to sustain them, and viewed small harbours. We spoke of John Constable who had painted these wide open skies and given them to the world. We visited a National Trust nature reserve, went to an otter reserve, watched with fascination as the keepers fed them.

'All this, Ann, without currency problems, unfamiliar heat, airport delays, having to remember the passports.'

'If only our August weather was always so good.'

Each afternoon I fell asleep, being recharged for our evening saunter, while Ann sat with her watercolours in the bow window, painting the market place, the street that led to the greens and the sea, wistfully wishing she could have done better.

She bought me a pedometer so I could now measure

the distance we walked. One day we notched up two and a half miles, forty minutes of which was done without my resorting to a bench, low wall or car seat. I was jubilant.

In the evenings we sat in the candlelit dining room, finding fish and chicken on the menu, so I could keep to the diet recommended by the doctor. The fever had gone out of life, there was peace in our hearts and a knowledge that our tomorrows like our yesterdays were in God's hand. In the hands of Psalm 139 (*The Living Bible*):

You saw me before I was born.
Every day of my life was recorded in your book.
Every moment was laid out
Before a single day had passed.
How precious are your thoughts about me, O God!
They are innumerable
I can't even count them;
They outnumber the grains of sand
And when I wake up in the morning, you are still with me!

For a short period, until colder days arrived, I became a walking enthusiast, God's method of journeying for people, as flying was for birds, and swimming for fish. We couldn't blame God for motorway jams; they were not his idea. Walking reduced stress, built up stamina, improved circulation, lowered blood pressure, strengthened heart muscles. To walk slowly was to find flowers in the hedgerow, enjoy the views, have time to pass the time of day with strangers.

In *Anglicans for Renewal* I read a challenging article by Russ Parker, an Anglican clergyman, who had been put out of work for almost a year with a virus infection. A wise pastor had told him that 'the stops as well as the steps of a righteous man are ordered by the Lord'.

Stopping had been a struggle for him. 'I felt as if my

faith was so puny,' he wrote, 'and that my continued illness would signal my ineffectiveness to the Christian community and my imminent redundancy as a so-called conference speaker. In fact the stopping proved to be a rich time of getting into deep places within myself and within God. I would say it has been a major resource in my growth as a person.'

Working a short day, I had time to read unread books, to visit National Trust gardens, to write personal rather than business letters. One was to Ann:

> What a tough time you've had since 27 May – months in which you've had your whole life rescheduled – visiting me or caring for me at home.
>
> What happy memories you have given me of walks in the forest, wonderful meals in the garden, afternoon tea in lovely places; arriving home from hospital, gorgeous flower arrangements, snuggling up together, raspberries picked by you for breakfast, watching videos in the evening with honey sandwiches, going to church again with you.
>
> And how I've appreciated the watch! I'm so grateful to our loving God that you are there to hold my hand, pray for me, and offer these supports. And, God willing, I look forward to wonderful years ahead together.

I jotted down my ninth lesson:

Love yourself enough to take a break.

The Ninth Lesson

LOVE YOURSELF ENOUGH TO TAKE A BREAK

When David Watson died, his wife, Anne, gave me several books from his library. In *Letters to My Students*, by C.H. Spurgeon, David marked the following words:

The bow cannot always be bent without fear of breaking. Repose is as needful to the mind as sleep to the body. . . . Hence the wisdom and compassion of our Lord, when he said to his disciples, 'Let us go into the desert and rest a while.'

What! When the people are fainting? When the multitudes are like sheep without a shepherd? Does Jesus talk of rest? When Scribes and Pharisees, like grievous wolves, are rending the flock, does he take his followers on an excursion into a quiet resting place?

To tug the oar from day to day, like a galley-slave who knows no holidays, suits not mortal man. Mill-streams go on and on for ever, but we must have our pauses and our intervals. Who can help being out of breath when the race is continued without intermission?

Even beasts of burden must be turned out to grass occasionally; the very sea pauses at ebb and flow; earth keeps the Sabbath of the wintry months; and man, even when exalted to be God's ambassador, must rest or faint.

Christians ought to be celebrating constantly. We ought to be pre-occupied with parties, banquets, feasts and merriment. We ought to give ourselves over to veritable orgies of joy because we have been liberated from the fear of life and the fear of death. We ought to attract people to the church quite literally by the fun there is in being a Christian.

—*Robert Hotchkins, University of Chicago*

The days that make us happy, make us wise.

—*John Masefield*

Chapter Ten

Please help Edward, Lord, with his problems. He is frailer than I tend to remember, emotionally, less decisive, not so relaxed about what we do. Guide him about retiring from *Renewal*, etc, and where we should live.

Ann and I had been discussing the future. Against my former expectations my body was telling me that, at least for the present, I must take an indefinite break from work; dispose of my business interests. We could possibly move away from Crowborough, to Eastbourne or Devon, or to a cottage overlooking the sea in Cornwall, and do whatever retired people do. It would be hard to give up work, terribly hard, for if my body was ready for a change of pace, my emotions were not. Ann was unsure of what it would be like having me around every day. It was not easy to get the balance right between being with me and going out to see friends and to events for which I lacked the energy or inclination.

The reality was that I would return home after a couple of hours in the office utterly exhausted. Soon the business would decline, the circulation of the two magazines would slump and my authors who had been so understanding would grow understandably impatient. Often after a heart attack, a victim recovers better by returning to their normal occupation but I was still experiencing problems.

There was the embarrassment of collapsing in a Sunday morning service at All Saints. Fortunately, we were not in the main body of the church and reasonably close to an exit. We had been standing for a succession of modern hymns led enthusiastically by the music group when I passed out. Ann caught me and eased me into the pew. Someone summoned an ambulance. I recovered quickly but confidence plummeted. I found it easier to walk than stand in one place, and had to avoid even a short queue in somewhere like the post office.

My friend the Rev. John Eddison had written of how easy it is to persuade ourselves that 'for the sake of the work' we ought to stay on a little longer, whereas all the time what the work is needing is a fresh hand on the tiller. 'By holding on just a few months more than we should do, we can make things that much harder for our successor, for too often that final period is not one of advance, but at best one of marking time and at worst slipping back.'

In his book *The Last Lap*, which I invited him to write in the mid-1980s, John quotes that old saying which is thrown at children when they are refused a third helping of some favourite pudding. 'You must always rise from the table with an appetite.' He believes it applies equally to this matter of our career. 'If we postpone retirement beyond a certain point, we make the final break when it comes that much harder, and find it more difficult to settle happily into a new pattern of life and activity.'

Reluctantly I would retire, feeling like the boy denied the final helping of pudding. Without any second thoughts I knew I wanted Jane and Tony Collins, two former colleagues from Hodders, to take over the agency, the magazines, my staff, the offices. Prayerfully, hopefully, I approached them. They lived a few miles away in the historic village of Speldhurst, where Tony was a Reader in the parish church and Jane was actively engaged in ministry among women. I knew them before they were married, had attended their beautiful wedding, and had met their teenage daughters on various occasions.

Committed Christians, with wide-ranging editorial gifts, more than twenty years younger, they needed more office space just for their own book publishing company, Monarch. They had the experience to take over my business and run it with a sense of mission. We met and discussed the possibilities and implications. When they said, in answer to my question, that they would retain my staff, I worked out with David Hanes, my accountant, a painless means by which they could acquire ownership. It is a decision I have not regretted; all that has happened since has confirmed the rightness of it.

'We love to settle down in our customary ways,' wrote Dr Fosdick, a great preacher of a previous age. 'We put our minds to bed and tuck them in. But the forward-moving purposes of our living God are forever disturbing our response and forcing us to move.' God sometimes cries, 'Move on.' In my case it was, 'Move out,' and I did so with relief. With typical generosity, Tony and Jane and the folk invited Ann and me to office get-togethers, and some of the wives organised Sunday lunches in their homes where we would all gather.

For seven years Ann had been a Trustee of Burrswood, a Christian centre for healthcare and ministry, founded by Dorothy Kerin. Its chairman was Bishop John Perry, and its director, Dr Gareth Tuckwell. After some uncertain years in the 1970s they restored Burrswood to being a healing centre of the highest repute where medical staff and clergy ministered in Christ's name. We had worked together to launch *Healing and Wholeness*.

'A heart attack is like a bereavement,' Gareth Tuckwell said sitting in our lounge after encouraging me to talk about my fears and aspirations. 'You're grieving the loss of your health, your work. It's natural. The grieving process has to be lived through. There's no escape. Hold on. Be patient. Things will improve.'

I told him of mental abberations, of writing the wrong month on letters, forgetting to sign a cheque, of not remembering where I left my car.

'Your difficulties are almost certainly temporary,' he said. 'Your doctor could prescribe medication but probably won't want to as most people recover as speedily without. Don't despair.'

I waved him off in his car wishing everyone had the privilege to spend an hour or more talking with such a wise doctor and Christian counsellor. He came unsought, sent I believe by God, and I found reassurance in his words, fresh purpose not to worry about trifling troubles, to keep a sense of perspective. The tunnel had a light at the end.

And then I had the dream.

I can recall every detail. I had been shopping in Tunbridge Wells and returned to the multi-storey car park to collect my car. Up the concrete steps to the dimly lit second floor, I glimpse at the boot protruding a little, near the top of the second row. To my astonishment and alarm I see through the window a crumpled man in a raincoat slumped in the front passenger seat of my car. His head is sagging on his chest. I cannot see his face. Has he broken in? Surely a car thief wouldn't be sitting there – or was he a drunk?

I fumble in my jacket pocket for the key. It's a dead man, I think, reluctant to accept the implications. How did he enter? The doors are locked, the windows closed. I have not left it that long. Less than the two hours on my ticket.

I open the driver's door in a sweat, careful not to bang it against the car alongside. 'Who are you? What are you doing here?' I ask. Getting no reply, I lean over the driver's seat to get a glimpse of the face of this crumpled figure, knowing if he's dead I shouldn't touch him until the police arrive.

'What are you doing in . . .?' It's pointless. I know he's dead. Gently with the tips of my fingers, I move his head so I can see his face.

It's me.

I freeze. Other motorists pass with their Marks and Spencer shopping bags, clutching their children, watching out for vehicles that might be reversing. I retreat out of the car in a state of shock, scared, unable to move my eyes from the sagging, lifeless form.

I am staring at me, a poor pathetic shape in a council car park. What a miserable place to die. No evidence of life, no record of last words, no indication of the cause of death, no witnesses. What happened? I perspire.

At that moment I woke up, silently crying out, seeking reassurance I was alive, in my own bed, my own home. Was this a premonition of death? Was I being given a final opportunity to put my heart, my affairs in order, of preparing to meet my God? I had seen my own lifeless body.

I had discussed with Ann, light-heartedly, the two hymns I would like at my funeral: 'Be Still My Soul' to Finlandia, and at its conclusion 'O Love That Will Not Let Me Go'. We'd examined our wills to see if they needed to be updated. I reached out to the small alarm clock on the bedside table. Almost 4 am. I wanted to share the dream with Ann, to wake her up, to see if she could explain its significance, to get two mugs of tea and talk it through. My mouth framed her name but no sound came. It would be unforgivably cruel to disturb her with this nightmare. It would scare her, whatever pretence she made for my benefit and she had known sufficient stress in recent months.

But I must tell somebody, seek an answer to the questions that choked me. Maybe Andrew Cornes, or John Hobbs, or Gareth Tuckwell. Not Ann, although she was the one I wished to tell most of all, in whom I constantly confided.

There were of course biblical records of God speaking to people through dreams. In his dream Jacob saw a ladder reaching up into heaven, the angels of God ascending and descending. Joseph both dreamed and interpreted Pharaoh's dreams, while Ezekiel dreamed of the valley of dry bones. On the Day of Pentecost, when the Christian Church was born, the Apostle Peter quoted the words of Joel, 'Your young men will see visions, your old men will dream dreams.'

As dawn broke the body in the car was more real to me than the bed, the bedside table, the wardrobe, the long mirror. I stared at the passenger, head resting on his chest, unable to quench my shock.

Was the dream the surfacing of a buried fear? Or a privileged warning? Or inconsequential? After breakfast I wrote down the detail, although I would never forget it, and told no one. Perhaps I was going to die. I had almost done so twice; perhaps next time it would be final.

'Maybe death is a gift, a blessing, a ceasing from a struggle and pain, as sleep is,' Luci Shaw had written in *God in the Dark*. 'We've been conditioned to think of death as an enemy, but that's because we, the survivors, haven't gone through its doorway, and all we know of it is what's on this side of the road – the loss, separation, grieving. For the one who dies in Christ, it is an opening to a new unimaginable world of life and light and knowledge.'

At the funeral of her husband Harold, Luci invited Myrna White to sing. Her words echoed round the church:

> Neither life nor death shall ever
> From the Lord his children sever,
> Unto them his grace he showeth
> And their sorrows all he knoweth.

Dr Kenneth Taylor paraphrased 1 Corinthians 15:42–44 in *The Living Bible*: 'The bodies we have now embarrass us for they become sick and die; but they will be full of glory when we come back to life again. Yes, they are weak, dying bodies now, but when we come back to life again they will be full strength. They are just human bodies at death, but when they come back they will be superhuman bodies. For just as there are natural, human bodies, there are also supernatural, spiritual bodies.

'The bodies we have now embarrass us for they become sick and die.' My recent limitations were an embarrassment – when women with their shopping, fifteen or twenty years older, passed me as I walked home up the modest hill from the newsagents; when I had to sit down while others stood; when I had to cancel the engagements in my diary. 'Weak, dying bodies now.'

For weeks I dragged the corpse round with me, the figure in the raincoat, telling no one, yet desperately wishing to ask someone what it meant. It was easier to share matters which didn't reveal my inner anxieties, hard to unlock the heart's door. I saw him in my waking moments, as I answered letters, plodded around the local roads, especially as I fell asleep. He did not lift his head, or move, or reply if I spoke. I would like to have buried him, but how? I sought comfort in Scripture: 'They are just human bodies at death, but when they come back they will be superhuman bodies. For just as there are natural, human bodies, there are also supernatural, spiritual bodies.'

Having lost my place in the working world it became imperative to establish somewhere at home, so we decorated the study. Ann did the ceiling, and over several days we stripped off the old wallpaper and over weeks pasted on the new. Once I would have done it all in a few hours. Ann made and lined the rich matching curtains, with handsome tie-backs, assisted in rearranging my books, making this room with the long view a place of refuge. I thanked God for it.

I took from the shelves Dr Paul Tournier's *A Place For You* which SCM Press had once allowed me to reprint. The author recognised the need of everyone to have 'somewhere to be'. He wrote:

> Man needs a place, and this need is vital to him. Where, then, does the need come from? I believe that in fact it is a manifestation of a need to live, to exist, to have a place in life. Life is not an abstraction. To exist is to occupy a particular living-space to which one has a right. This is true even of animals.

Through life our places change, sometimes brutally, sometimes gradually. The Bible tells us that it has been so since time began, since the first created couple were moved from the Garden of Eden, since Abraham was told to move on at an age when he thought he was settled for life. We do not know where our place will be tomorrow but with the Psalmist we can say, 'You are my place of safety.'

'God with us' was the theme at our church that Christmas. With us in health or in weakness, with us in prosperity or poverty, with us in triumph or failure. Jesus born to be with us – in this world and the world to come. He had a place for us here, and there he had prepared a place where 'death shall be no more, neither shall there be mourning nor crying nor pain any more' (Rev 21:4, RSV).

It was a joyful season, with visitors young and old dropping in for meals, exchanging gifts, playing games, pulling crackers. And for the New Year, Ruth Fowke came, as she often did at this time of year, to spend a few days with us. As Ruth was a friend, psychiatrist and counsellor I knew I had found someone I could talk with about my dream. We were sitting in the lounge together, Ann busy downstairs in the kitchen.

'Ruth, may I share with you a dream I had? It's puzzled me. I need someone to tell me its meaning. You'll soon understand why I haven't asked Ann, why I daren't.'

'I'm not sure I can help but I'll be glad to listen.' Putting down the magazine she was reading she turned to face me. Ruth has counselled hundreds of depressed, worried people, advised clergy, missionaries. Some of them must have spoken about their dreams.

'Was it a recent dream?'

'This autumn. I wanted to tell Ann but thought it would be unkind.'

She didn't take her eyes off me as I spoke, and listened without interruption as I described in detail what I had seen, the picture vividly ingrained.

'I can appreciate why you didn't mention it to Ann,' she said, when I finished, listening to make sure she was still in the kitchen.

'What does it mean, Ruth? If anything.' Suddenly I

felt foolish for giving a dream any weight. She replied soberly, thoughtfully, choosing each word carefully. She didn't dismiss the possibility of it being a premonition of death, it might be, but thought it unlikely. God didn't normally indicate personal forthcoming events like this. There were days and seasons only he knew. Instead, he quietly prepared us for them. She would have been praying as she listened, one ear tuned to me, one to God.

'I can't be sure what it indicates,' she said reflectively, a lifetime of experience behind her. 'You said you stood outside the car, detached from the figure inside. You looked at the body which was you and yet you were alive, an observer, able to walk away from the scene if you wished. I don't know, but I wonder if the self you saw in the car was the part of you which has died.'

'How do you mean?'

'Your health? Your publishing? Tony and Jane taking over *Renewal*, the agency?'

'You mean, Ruth, it's about the me that has died? Things I identified with, for which I no longer have a responsibility? On which I should close the door and walk away?'

She nodded. 'Yes, maybe.'

Her explanation found a welcome echo in my heart. Perhaps it made sense because I wished it that way, but reviewed even critically it seemed right. Parting with my business was a form of dying. There was a future but I would not be part of it. The publications, the authors would no longer be carried in the seat of my car. I had died to one adventure and God might have a fresh one in store.

'With that explanation I think I could share the dream with Ann. I'd like to. A dozen times I've almost mentioned it.'

She said she thought I should. Shortly we heard Ann coming with a tray of freshly made tea and cakes. She poured the tea.

'Ann, I was telling Ruth about a dream I had. Asking for her explanation. I found the dream rather frightening but Ruth has made it seem less so. I wanted to tell you first but didn't want to alarm you. I've written it down. Would you like to read it? I handed her two typewritten sheets, hoping she wouldn't be hurt because I'd confided in Ruth before her.

She gulped as she read, made no comment, went on reading. Then she reached out to me.

I told her Ruth's likely explanation.

'I'm glad you spoke to Ruth first,' she said softly. 'I'd have been terribly worried otherwise.'

She reread what I had written. 'But do you think you're going to die?'

'One day, not yet. But sooner than I would have done, without a heart attack. But life's uncertain for us all and who knows I might outlive you. I'm not sure I'd want that. And we might both outlive Ruth.' I grinned at her. 'Sorry, Ruth.'

She smiled. 'Anyone like a game of Scrabble?' There were more important things in life than dreams.

My first public engagement after Barnstaple was to participate briefly in the funeral service of a fellow church member, Dr James Broomhall. A former leader of the China Inland Mission and Overseas Missionary Fellowship, he had spent his retirement writing six full-length volumes covering the missionary history of China. The final volume which told of James Hudson Taylor's ministry was *It Is Not Death To Die*.

John Bunyan had first put those words into the mouth of Valiant-for-Truth. Dr Broomhall's daughter asked if I would read Bunyan's words at the funeral service.

My sword I give to him who shall succeed me
in my pilgrimage,
and my courage and skill to him that can get it.
My marks and scars I carry with me
to be a witness that I have fought his battles,
who now will be my rewarder.
'Death, where is thy sting? . . .
Grave, where is thy victory?'
So he passed over,
And all the trumpets sounded for him
on the other side,
'It is not death to die!'

Dr Broomhall had a complete confidence in that triumphant exclamation of faith. So did I. 'God,' I prayed, 'give me such a hunger for what you have prepared for those who love you, that I will not wish to remain in this troubled world longer than you desire.'

My tenth lesson was:

It is not death to die.

The Tenth Lesson

IT IS NOT DEATH TO DIE

For we know that when this tent we live in now is taken down – when we die and leave these bodies – we will have new bodies in heaven. . . . How weary we grow of our present bodies. That is why we look forward eagerly to the day when we shall have heavenly bodies which we shall put on like new clothes.

—2 Corinthians 5:1–19 (The Living Bible)

Heaven is the goal of man, and heaven gives the true perspective for our present life.

—Archbishop Michael Ramsey

Jesus said, 'I am the resurrection and the life; he who believes in me, though he die, yet shall he live, and whoever lives and believes in me shall never die.'

—John 11:25,26 (RSV)

The morning before he was executed by the Nazis, Dietrich Bonhoeffer sent a final message to his friend Bishop George Bell: 'Tell him that for me this is the end but also the beginning.'

Death is the great adventure, beside which moon landings and space trips pale into insignificance.

—Joseph Bayley

Chapter Eleven

Spring came to my heart early in the New Year and I was able for the first time to appreciate the cards and letters which had been sent the previous summer. There must have been at least 200 with some lovely handmade ones from children. I read and reread them all.

Andrew Cornes, our vicar, in a loving letter to us in Barnstaple, had quoted Lamentations 3:25,26 – 'The Lord is good to those who wait for him, to the soul that seeks him. It is good that one should wait quietly for the salvation of the Lord.' He commented, 'You will inevitably be doing a lot of waiting over the next weeks but I know that you and Ann will be waiting not just for your health to return, but waiting for the Lord.'

Carolyn Armitage, a former Hodder colleague, sent a card, 'Don't follow the (probably apocryphal) example of David Adeney, who escaped out of a hospital window to attend a conference!'

Dr Maxwell Jones, and his wife Do, reminded me of his recovery from a heart attack and kidney failure and quoted Psalm 73:26 – 'My flesh and my heart faileth: but God is the strength of my heart, and my portion for ever.'

From Edinburgh, the Rev. Derek Prime, an author

with whom I had been associated for twenty-five years, quoted Faber's hymn:

> Ill that he blesses is our good,
> And unblest good is ill;
> And all is right that seems most wrong,
> If it be his sweet will.

A London doctor, Gaius Davies, inscribed his card, 'Get well slowly,' while a publisher from America, Dr Victor Oliver, commented: 'We have just received news of your illness. There are pros and cons; you are in Devon, with Ann, and probably having clotted cream with strawberries (perhaps a little early for that), and perhaps most importantly it will necessitate two to three months of rest and relaxation, and opportunity for meditation. Take time to smell the roses, as we say in America.'

And there was a long letter from my office. Each member of the staff wrote half a page sharing news about their families, holidays, events of interest, not once mentioning work. Penny Thomas asked, 'Do you like rhubarb? Well I thought I did until this morning. Not one to miss a bargain, I purchased some cheap and cheerful sticks of the stuff which my sister-in-law helpfully offered to cook. Unhelpfully, she must have forgotten the sugar – believe me it doesn't taste like the same fruit.' She went on, 'On a sweeter note our family is very proud of my brother, who has returned from Florence with two gold medals, having taken part in an international regatta for the disabled.' Helen Nicholson, her colleague, shared a joke she had been told about a rabbi who went to the synagogue every Sabbath. Every week they had a lottery and the rabbi was keen to win it. The first Sabbath he prayed hard that God would let him win, but when the result was announced it wasn't him.

The second Sabbath, the lottery was run again, and he prayed harder, on his knees: 'God, I really need the money, please let me win.' Still he didn't win. The third Sabbath he implored God to let him win, reminding him how much he needed the money, and then he paused. In the quiet, a voice came down to him: 'Meet me half way, can't you? Buy a ticket!'

The theme of many greetings was summed up in the words, 'We are what we have been; we're to become what we're not.' Something possible only by the grace of God.

I was learning that one doesn't have to be successful to be loved, that we are loved by God and our friends in spite of our triumphs or lack of them. In Luci Shaw's *Life Path*, she tells how she was asked for a definition of 'success'.

> I believe that a measure of success is essential in the formula for human living. But the more I think about it, the more I am convinced that succeeding (in the commonest sense of that word) may be either destructive or healthy, depending on what motivates it. Our culture urges us, always, to do better, to be better, to be competitive, to win the pennant, to take home the biggest Christmas bonus, to pick up a Pulitzer or at least to raise the most self-confident children. Such success is nearly always pride and ambition centred.
>
> And it's addictive. Achievers need a regular 'success fix'.
>
> Does the Bible endorse success? Yes, but of a different kind. In spite of adversity, Joseph climbed the success ladder not because he was aggressive and pushy but 'because the Lord was with him and made him prosper', and 'gave him success in everything he did.' . . . When we are moved upon by God to be obedient, and achieve a goal that furthers his kingdom, success has an eternal dimension.

What a price we pay for our earthly gains. Surrey, which has more than its share of high-achievers has also, according to the Mother's Union, Europe's highest divorce rate. Workaholics Anonymous claims that up to ten per cent of British people are addicted to their work – and the habit is as difficult to kick as alcohol or drugs. Professor Cary Cooper of the University of Manchester Intitute of Science and Technology tells people in management, 'If you drive yourself to a heart attack, the business will carry on without you. The company will say, "Sorry, Fred," but they will survive.'

Rob Parsons, in *The Sixty Minute Father*, reflects, 'No-one was ever heard to say on his death bed, "I wish I had spent more time at the office."'

Richard Foster, author of *The Celebration of Discipline*, sitting in our lounge one sunny afternoon, told how he came to realise that he did not have to spend his life in adding more and more duties to an already busy schedule. He had to let go of the need always to say yes, to be free from the burden that everybody must have a good opinion of him. To seek first God's kingdom. He advocated keeping a record of all activities for a month then ranking them in the following way. 1. Absolutely essential. 2. Important but not essential. 3. Helpful but not necessary. 4. Trivial. He says we should eliminate the last two of the four categories and twenty per cent of the first two. We could cut out a great deal of activity without affecting our service.

According to a report by Ruth Gledhill in *The Times*, Rev. Clifford Bowman, a married rector in Worksop, carried out a survey among clergy asking 300 questions about their physical health, the burden of administration, family life, the ability to delegate, etc. Fifty-nine per cent said they had no social life, and more than eighty per cent said the abnormal hours they worked were a cause of marital tensions and admitted their home lives were suffering because of the stress. In some cases vicars' wives had amended the questionnaire. Where the vicar had said their jobs did not cause stress, the wives had scribbled: 'Oh yes it does.'

John Pollock, in his biography *Moody without Sankey*, tells how as Moody grew older there were more and more calls for his evangelistic campaigns. Phrases like 'the load is heavy at times' were frequently on his lips. A Harley Street specialist confirmed slight heart trouble and asked how often he preached.

'Oh, I usually preach three times a day. On Sundays four or five.'

'How many days a week?'

'Six, but during the winter seven.'

'You're a fool, sir, you're a fool. You're killing yourself.'

Pollock tells us that a Chicago friend of Moody expected that he might hear at any time of his sudden death. Moody's response was, 'We must grow or go to the wall,' and, 'Let us push out in all directions.' To Dr F. B. Meyer he said, 'God is marching on and I must keep pace with him.'

Soon after he died.

There were now few entries in my diary; an occasional preaching engagement at All Saints, or something like a Salvation Army event for the officers at Sunbury Court, or a meeting of the Governors at SPCK in London. A trip to London was always followed by a relaxing day. As one of the lay pastors in my church I found myself visiting those who were facing difficult times, and over a period being alongside several older men who were dying at home or in hospital – an enormous privilege.

I was learning about life's limitations and its opportunities and, of course, at times I was frustrated. I prayed, 'Teach me, Lord, to discover the opportunities within my limitations rather than to fret because of them. Enable me to see the possibilities which were not present when I was in a busy job.'

I thought of those who had lost their sight, or never had it; of those confined to wheelchairs; of some who were unhappily married but believed it right to stay with their partner and children. 'Lord, I have so much, my limitations are so small, so please forgive me for complaining, for negative thoughts.'

I thought of how Pastor Richard Wurmbrand had spent three years in solitary confinement in a cell thirty feet below ground in Bucharest for preaching the gospel. During that time he was cut off from all communication with the outside world.

'To be in a solitary cell under the communists or the Nazis,' he told me, 'is to reach the peak of suffering. The reactions of Christians who pass through such trial are something apart from everything else.' Face to face with his own soul, in conditions of extreme stress made worse by beatings, doping and torture, what had he done to retain his sanity, I asked.

'I had no Bible, no books, no writing paper, but I prepared a fresh sermon each day and every evening delivered it to an imaginary congregation – sometimes to God, or the angels.'

Did Jesus Christ feel limited in this earthly ministry: with no computer, no fax, no telephone, no television studio, a handful of unreliable disciples, ministering in one tiny corner of the world? Did he dream of visiting Rome, preaching a sermon in the amphitheatre, of writing a treatise that would become the official handbook for his followers in future generations? No, the New Testament indicates he was content to do the will of God, only those things which his Father said.

After a further unexpected spell in hospital, it was arranged that I should have an angioplasty to clear two partly blocked arteries. It meant an overnight stay in a London clinic but proved to be no great trial and I remained awake to watch the proceedings on a television set. Thirty per cent of patients have to return a second time after six months or subsequently have open-heart surgery. I experienced the benefit of angioplasty with no subsequent call-back, although I was in hospital again soon afterwards for unrelated surgery.

Eighteen months after Barnstaple I was fit enough to go with Ann for a week's winter break in Puerto de la Cruz in the Canaries. In contrast to the freezing temperatures at home the weather started warm and sunny. One window in our hotel room overlooked the sea, the other Mount Teide. On the third morning, when I drew back the curtain and glanced out, the volcanic mountain was covered with heavy clouds, surrounded by mist.

'Not a good day,' I said to Ann. 'Well, we can't expect every day to be perfect.'

'Look out of the other window,' she advised.

I crossed the room and did. On the coast it was going to be another glorious day. After that, we said laughingly each morning, 'Look out of the other window.'

I included the thought that we should always do so in a Sunday evening sermon at All Saints. The rich farmer was a man who spent all his time gazing through one window; at his barns, his possessions, his achievements, his ambition to build bigger and better barns. A Christian, I suggested, is one who has learned to look through two windows, for there is another world, another life, another kingdom. He does not neglect his family, his home, his barns, his business, the responsibilities God has given him in this life, but when he reads his Bible, or goes to church, he is taking a look through the other – more important – window.

I told of the woman who awoke at 3 am exhausted,

fearful, unable to sleep. She believed God whispered to her that night: 'Stop dwelling on the problems and start studying the promises.' She turned on the light and reached for her Bible: 'Be careful for nothing; but in everything by prayer and supplication with thanksgiving let your requests be made known unto God' (Philippians 4:6, AV).

'Look through the other window,' was in my mind as I searched through a cuttings file at home for an article I had once written for *Renewal* about Jackie Pullinger. Jackie had been a friend since I published her book *Chasing the Dragon* about life within the notorious Walled City in Hong Kong. *The South China Post* aptly called her 'The Angel of the Walled City'.

During her early years in the East, Jackie had been to see a house in Kowloon thinking it might be a residence for drug addicts who needed release from their addiction. She took a friend to view it. The premises were in a bad state, heaps of rubble everywhere, and nowhere to cook.

'There's not even a lavatory,' her companion said, bursting into tears. 'No one can live here.'

Jackie gazed at it. 'All I could see was glory,' she recalled. 'God had opened my eyes. I saw a different house. My friend saw the rubbish. I knew I was meant to take it. God can give us resurrection eyes for the things that he wants us to hope for, the jobs we're meant to be doing. We'll then see them in a way no one else can. "It's really silly working there," others may say. "There's no chance of success. Nobody will ever believe in Jesus. You're just wasting your time."'

Jackie's reply to such statements was, 'They are seeing with natural eyes. We're seeing with our new eyes, like the two men on the road to Emmaus, whose eyes were opened so they recognised the stranger who accompanied them.'

I had been to Hong Kong with Ann. Afraid to enter alone, we had been escorted into the Walled City – now demolished – to see where she had once lived and found that resurrection eyes had truly coloured all of Jackie's ministry. When she looked into the semi-darkness of the alleyways, where half a million people were packed into an area of half a square mile, with drips from the floor above, and garbage running down the centre, she saw it all with God-given eyes.

I prayed for new eyes, eyes which saw the hosts of God encamped around; eyes which let down the nets at his command, even where apparently there were no fish; eyes which discovered 'the light shines in the darkness, and the darkness has not overcome it' (John 1:4,5, RSV); eyes which see the realities hidden from the human eye.

My eleventh lesson became a fresh longing that God would enable me to

See the world with resurrection eyes.

SEE THE WORLD WITH RESURRECTION EYES

When he was at the table with them, he took bread . . . and began to give it to them. Then their eyes were opened and they recognised him.

—*Luke 24:30,31 (NIV)*

Their eyes were opened, and then they saw who it was, and knew him well enough. The mists were scattered, the veil was taken off, and then they made no question but it was their Master. He might put on one shape or another, but no other could put on his; and therefore it must be he. See how Christ by his Spirit and grace makes himself known. The work is completed by the opening of the eyes of their mind.

—*Matthew Henry*

God our Father, Creator of all,
Today is the day of Easter joy.
May the risen Lord
Breathe on our minds and open our eyes
That we may know him in the breaking of bread,
And follow him in the risen life.

—*The Liturgy of the Hours*

Open my eyes, that I may behold wondrous things out of thy law.

—*Psalm 119:18 (RSV)*

And immediately he received his sight and followed him.

—*Mark 10:52 (RSV)*

Teach me, my God and King,
In all things thee to see.

—*George Herbert*

Chapter Twelve

If in 1993 the shutters were closed on areas of my life, by summer 1996 they were opening again. A new dawn was breaking. On a limited scale I was ready for action and longing for it. According to the British Heart Foundation, heart attack victims can end up in a vicious circle of fear. 'That fear leads to physical inactivity; a weaker heart muscle and a growing belief that returning to work means returning to a death sentence.' I had known that fear. Now it was a matter of holding on to all I had been struggling to learn while being open to fresh opportunities. To work, yet to have freedom to spend a day by the sea in the middle of the week, or to rest in the afternoon for an hour. I had reached retiring age. 'But I think I'd rather die working than sitting in an armchair,' I told Ann. 'I need those resurrection eyes to discover what that work is.'

I pondered when walking on Ashdown Forest, or as the first light came through the curtains with birdsong from the garden. 'For God alone my soul waits in silence,' the Psalmist wrote, 'for my hope is from him.' In the silence I endeavoured to be attentive to any pointer to the future, meanwhile serving on two or three committees.

I used my leisure to read a wide variety of books. One

or two novels, including David Gutterson's *Snow Falling on Cedars* which one reviewer described as a 'tender examination of fairness and forgiveness'; many biographies, the most rewarding being *Dickens*, a 600-page life by Fred Kaplin; and some travel books. One Christian title I appreciated was *Space for God* written by David Runcorn, whom I had known as senior chaplain at Lee Abbey in the 1980s. His words about the commas and full stops in our life were thought-provoking, memorable:

> The purpose of punctuation in a piece of writing is to guide the reader into the true meaning of words and phrases; through it we understand. . . . Punctuation is a helpful way of thinking about Jesus' relationship with silence and solitude. Jesus punctuated his life with silence and solitude. His times alone were the commas, pauses and full stops in the story of his life. They gave the rest of his life its structure, direction and balance. His words and his works were born out of those hours of silent waiting upon God.

I had trudged through three years of commas, pauses and long full stops. Now, while remembering the punctuation, I was to begin a fresh chapter, a chapter of which only God knew the length.

It started with a generous birthday book token from Ann – one pound for every year of my life. I was glad I was not twenty-five and on that day I would have been content to be one hundred! Looking at the colourful jackets in a window of Waterstone's bookshop in Tunbridge Wells, the tokens fairly sizzling in my pocket, the thought came of starting a Christian publishing house issuing books written only by women to compensate for the overwhelming dominance of male authors in my career. Someone would later describe it as a kind of death-bed repentance. I would have to say sorry Billy Graham, sorry Michael Green, sorry George Carey. I would be open to publish for their wives.

I considered a partnership with an established Christian publisher, suggesting a separate division with its own imprint, but most of them were going through a time of retrenchment and painful redundancies, their warehouses overflowing with slow-moving titles. Perhaps I should launch it, then hand it over after a couple of years when I had demonstrated the possibilities.

Stop! The lights ahead turned red. Apply the brakes. Would such a venture be a negation of all the lessons I had been struggling to master, a return to the old life of deadlines and commercial pressures from which I had been delivered? Would I be driving myself to another heart attack? Was I trying to resurrect the lifeless body in the passenger seat of the car? What about the lessons God had been so forcibly teaching me? I had taken an involuntary break, a long one: should it be a permanent way of life?

If I did proceed, could I discipline myself to take time off, to work short hours, to have a fun day each week, to love Ann and myself enough to take a break in the middle of a working day, to go out for coffee or drive to a National Trust property for lunch? Could I ever hope to live out my lessons in a publishing situation? I didn't know. If only I were wiser, could be sure of God's will.

It might be safer to learn to play golf, to get involved in further voluntary work, to join some more committees. There were plenty of opportunities for good works and we were surrounded by golf enthusiasts who offered to impart their skills.

I moped around for a week searching my heart, knowing how easy it is to deceive oneself. 'The heart of man is deceitfully wicked,' Jesus said. It is amazingly simple to do what one wishes, then to find a rational, plausible explanation. And a Bible verse to support it.

But the idea persisted of launching a company specialising in Christian books by women; of finding new unpublished talent. Day and night it would not go away.

I cannot be sure my decision was right, there was no blinding revelation, but eventually it seemed right to proceed – while endeavouring to hold fast to all that God had been showing me. A wave of enthusiasm instantly replaced my doubts. The world became a place of infinite possibility. I was young again, walking through summer meadows, creating something. The view to the forest from my study shimmered in the sun.

'Let's do it together,' Ann said bravely when I shared my decision with her that evening.

'You could be an editor,' I replied.

'Go for it,' said David Hanes, a senior partner in a firm of Christian accountants, when we outlined the proposal to him two weeks later.

'We'd like you to be one of the directors,' we said. He suggested a source of additional capital. David had been my financial mentor when I published *Renewal*, Highland Books, and ran the agency. A good accountant is to a business what a good minister is to a church. Indispensable.

We decided to call it the Christina Press and initially it would be run from two rooms at home, calling on outside resources. David Nickalls, of Bookprint Creative Services in Eastbourne, agreed to produce the books; Kingsway Communications to market them to the bookshops, and STL in Carlisle to distribute them. Tony Collins, as always full of wise counsel, introduced me to a freelance copy-editor, Alison Graham. Marion Cameron, a gifted member of All Saints was willing to provide secretarial assistance, using a room in her home and her husband Don's computer.

A publisher must have books to publish and we had none, but a press release about the launch of Christina

Press changed that. Our postman wondered what had happened – was every day a birthday? The thick brown envelopes, the neatly wrapped parcels, poured in. Most had already been rejected by other publishers or were unwanted collections of poetry. The thoughtful would-be authors sent return postage and we wrote a personal letter to each. Printed rejection slips are unkind.

When we had all in place – except the books – I returned from an SPCK committee in London to be greeted by Ann grasping an unsolicited manuscript *Precious to God* by Sarah Bowen.

'Read this,' she said. 'I'll get you a cup of tea while you do. I couldn't put it down. She's a very special mother and she writes beautifully.'

I looked at the address. I did not know anyone in Stafford and had not heard the author's name. I sank into an easy chair and started to turn the pages not stopping until I had finished the book, several times blinking away a tear.

Sarah and her husband, delighted to be starting a family, had their expectations shattered by the arrival of a severely handicapped child; and then another. They faced difficulties which would have rocked any family. Yet their home (and the book) was full of laughter and love.

One evening, as the dog and I returned from a walk, entering the little yard to reach the back door, all I could hear was both children crying and moaning. Oh, no, I thought, I can't stand any more. I can't face going in. So I opened the back door and said to Dick, 'I'm not coming in, I'm going. I've had enough.'

With that I shut the door and walked off. Seconds later, Dick was by my side, and grasping my hand he said, 'Hang on, wait for me, I'm coming with you.'

We looked at each other and started to laugh, had a hug and then went back into the house and carried on.

Two hours after returning from London I phoned Sarah to say we would be privileged to publish her book, that a contract would be sent immediately. This was the start of a gentle flow of good books.

Later, the reviewers would respond as enthusiastically to *Precious to God* as we had done. *The New Christian Herald* was typical! 'What a gem of a book. . . . As Sarah and her husband come to terms with the tragedy that befalls them they find God and learn he is there for them all.' *Woman Alive* would publish an extract, *Healing and Wholeness* a full-length feature, and enquiries would come from overseas publishers.

Our first books appeared in spring 1997. The major event of the year, however, the fulfilment of a dream, came in the autumn when we published jointly with the Bible Reading Fellowship *Day by Day with God*, the first regular dated Bible reading notes written for women.

The bridge between Christina Press and the BRF was Shelagh Brown, the editor of BRF's *New Daylight*. Over lunch Ann and I shared with Shelagh, a friend of mine for years, our idea for this unique publication and volunteered that because of the potential it would be best for us to do it jointly with an established Bible reading organisation. She suggested the BRF. We said yes if, in addition to her existing commitments, she would also edit *Day by Day with God*.

'You would bring together the writers, and have the editorial oversight of the publication,' I said.

Her response was immediate and enthusiastic. She was aware that most women, in most churches, do not read the Bible and believed that the needs of these women had not been fully grasped.

'Although men and women are both made in God's image, in many ways it is only a woman who can understand what it means and feels like to be a woman. And in some respects we learn differently from men,' she said. 'We'll target the women who read little apart from magazines.'

It was a long lunch and she had to cancel a dental appointment. She proposed to BRF a partnership with us and when they said yes she persuaded, as only Shelagh could, a group of women to write on a regular basis. They included Celia Bowring, Rosemary Green, Jennifer Rees Larcombe, Hilary McDowell, Bridget Plass and Mary Reid. For me, an additional bonus was the birth of a friendship with Richard Fisher, BRF's Chief Executive.

When the contributors were in place, I had a relaxed lunch with Shelagh and Richard in London before going with Ann on holiday to Norway. Since my heart attack I had been only to cities and resorts where good medical facilities were on hand but now we opted for a trip to the Arctic where there would be less easy access to facilities like a coronary care unit.

My spirits soared when we arrived in Bergen, the gateway to Norway. While we waited for the flight to Trondheim, I spotted an unexpected sign. 'Look at that,' I whispered to Ann, pointing out the inscription: 'This is a silent airport.' With aircraft arriving and departing every fifteen minutes or so it was a brave claim, but inside the terminal was sound-proofed, amazingly quiet, with no piped music, no announcements about arrivals and departures, no verbal warnings about not leaving luggage unattended.

The mountains and lakes of Norway, the silent places, are among its chief attractions for those of us who live in a noisy world, where in spite of technology, and sometimes because of it, the blare and roar of everyday life intensifies. Ask anyone who lives near a main road. Ask anyone who attends a noisy church. Maybe we have something to learn from the Quakers. Richard Foster wrote in *Celebration of Discipline*:

> To still the activity of the flesh so that the activity of the Holy Spirit dominates the way we live will affect and inform public worship. Sometimes it will take the form of absolute silence. Certainly it is more fitting to come in reverential silence and awe before the Holy One of Eternity than to rush into his presence with hearts and minds askew and tongues full of words. The scriptural admonition is, 'The Lord is in this holy temple; let all the earth keep silence before him.' (Hab 2:20)

There is a time for making 'a joyful noise to the Lord'; there is an honoured place for choirs and music groups, for gifted musicians and cheerful voices, but we are impoverished if we neglect to keep silence before God.

Once we had broken away from our travelling companions there was ample opportunity for quiet in Norway, whether in a dim corner of Trondheim Cathedral, or on the Lofoten Islands where we stayed in a 'rorbu' or fisherman's hut. Ann and I missed one highly recommended tour to stay with the birds and the shoals of fish which swam within yards of our accommodation.

A highlight of the early part of our holiday was the ten-hour journey, along the longest stretch of railway line in Norway, passing through tiny hamlets, alongside lakes, and up snow-covered mountains. The area known as Nordland is Norway's second largest county and is aptly said to have 'lots of weather'. We were spectators of it. We travelled on the first of the two daily trains from Trondheim, passing through rich sunny farmlands towards barren mountains. After four or five hours the countryside became increasingly harsh, with mountains of 6,000 feet, and the second largest glacier in Norway. After eight hours we reached the Arctic Circle where, at the highest point, we were surrounded by deep snow.

There was a rush to the window to see our first reindeer. In the winter a train had been snowed in here for three days, a helicopter bringing in food and warm clothing.

The island town of Tromso, known as the gateway to the North Pole, was our furthest point from home. Here it was completely light at midnight and in the winter was dark at mid-day. As we entered the recently completed cathedral we were handed printed prayers inviting us to reflect on the God who created and loves us; to reflect on Jesus Christ who died and rose again from the dead for us. I treasured this prayer:

> Lord, fill me with your Spirit.
>> Take away all disturbance, unawareness and chill.
> Let my eyes see, my ears hear, my tongue speak,
>> my innermost being become silent.
> Hear kindly my prayer and have mercy on me.
>> For Jesus Christ's sake.

Our minds were filled with rich, peaceful pictures as we arrived back at Gatwick airport to be met by Rod and Margaret, good friends, for the half-hour drive home. When we had taken the luggage from the boot, they hesitantly handed me a letter from Marion Cameron.

'I'm afraid it contains some bad news,' Rod said gently. 'We thought it best not to give it to you until now.' I tore open the envelope, leaving the suitcases on the drive, Ann waiting to turn the key in the front door.

Shelagh Brown, our gifted new editor, had died after falling down the stairs of her Oxford home as she hurried to open the door to dinner guests. An operation at the Radcliffe hospital for a blood clot on the brain had not saved her.

Rod and Margaret gave us a hug and left. We stumbled indoors unable to believe it. Shelagh, always bubbling with vitality, with whom we were going to spend a weekend in Oxford, Shelagh who had been so key to *Day by Day with God*, Shelagh who had so much to offer, was no longer with us. Why, God, why?

I didn't want to remember what David Watson said: 'I've stopped asking God why, instead I'm learning to ask him what is he saying to me through this?' I only wanted to know what he was up to. How could a loving heavenly Father allow this?

We were exhausted after the long journey from Tromso, but a deeper tiredness overwhelmed us now. I was unwilling to accept the content of the letter. Instead I took a sleeping tablet, something I am reluctant to do, and went to bed. I didn't want to talk to God. It was a harsh thing that he had permitted to happen.

'I've fallen out with him,' I told Ann.

'I'm glad we didn't hear while we were in Norway,' she said.

I first met Shelagh when she was the personal assistant to a Hodder author, Sir Norman Anderson, then for a time she was in the press office at Buckingham Palace. In 1981 she was made a deaconess in the Anglican Church and was ordained in 1987. Her full potential was released when she became editor of *New Daybreak* and saw its circulation soar.

The Times in a long obituary described her as one of the best-known women priests and the 400 to 500 people at her funeral service in Oxford, including four Anglican bishops, confirmed that statement. As Bishop Gavin Reid said in his address, she did not know the meaning of no when approaching authors. But from her determination to sign them up came unexpected treasures, as busy people found time to share experiences and insights that she had decided should become public property.

She left no instructions as to the hymns and readings at her funeral but precise instructions as to what should be served at the reception to be held afterwards – *Lanson Black Label* champagne. It was to be a party for all those friends who one day she would meet again in heaven.

Her unexpected death created a serious crisis for us. The first issue of a dated publication is critical, setting the tone for the future, and she was not around to oversee it. From our home we had to get the contributions in from the nine writers she had chosen, edit them to the right length, check the Bible quotes, write headings, and hand them over to the BRF for printing and design within two weeks of the funeral – on top of our additional commitments. We had lost valuable time on holiday. Ann and I put aside everything so that *Day by Day with God* could be published on schedule. Letters remained unanswered, meals were simplified, Ann's medical journals left unread. We had to do it and several times thought it might prove impossible. Then we found ourselves being inspired by the material we were poring over. We read choice extracts out to each other.

'What about this, Ann?' I said, reading from a contribution by Alie Stibbe, a vicar's wife, who was introducing Brother Lawrence who went about barefoot. As a mother with young children she had often felt guilty because she could no longer find space for the traditional 'quiet time', then she discovered she could treat her kitchen floor as holy ground, dedicating to God the simple tasks she performed there; giving thanks to God as she stacked the dishwasher and took out the rubbish. For Wednesday 11 February she recommended:

> Go into your kitchen or place of work and take off your shoes. As you stand barefoot on the floor, ask God to bless and consecrate that place so that you can serve him there in his presence from now on. Spend the day barefoot, so that feeling the floor through the soles of your feet may constantly jog your mind back to God.

Assisted by our copy-editor, Alison Graham, we completed the editing at 12.30 pm in Sussex on the critical day and handed them over to Richard Fisher in London at 2.30 pm. I hope Shelagh would have been proud of us.

Mary Reid, one of Shelagh's dearest friends, was invited to succeed her as the editor. Mary, who had once edited *Family* magazine and had been involved in book publishing, to our joy accepted the invitation from Richard Fisher, Ann and myself. 'If God opens a door like this I believe I should go through it,' she said, not unmindful of her responsibilities as Bishop Gavin's wife. 'I'll give it a go.'

Day by Day with God was happily launched in November 1997. If we had survived without Shelagh it was not, I confess, without some loss of sleep. In spite of every good intention, I was rediscovering that there are periods when the impossible is demanded. We respond gallantly but we must decline to accept that as the norm. Listening to our body, learning to take a break, even coming to a full stop must be inbuilt into our pattern of living.

Nigel McCullough, the Bishop of Wakefield, in a Saturday Reflection in *The Times* wrote on 'Why we may need to do less for God'. I cut it out, and looked for a space to stick it on my study wall, thinking perhaps I should make copies for my friends.

The bishop quoted St Vincent de Paul in the seventeenth century who said, 'It is a trick of the Devil, which he employs to deceive good souls, to incite them to do more than they are able, in order that they may no longer be able to do anything.' From his wide experience of the Church he added, 'Mounting extra events is invariably the antithesis of what is required to bring people closer to an experience of God.'

It was a word for myself which I had to hold in balance

with what had been my motto for the year. Getting the balance right is inevitably problematic which brings me to the motto.

With our cards and prayer letters the previous Christmas came one from Luci (Shaw) and John Hoyte in California, giving an outline of their 1996 adventures.

> *January.* John and I joined over twenty-five Hoytes in the South Island of New Zealand for a family reunion. The older generation telling the younger 'how it was' in their youth in China, and in the prison camp. Memorable, moving accounts. In Queenstown many of us also did the bungy-jumping thing. I did a second jump (250 feet in Skipper's Gorge) when I learned I could get a senior discount. When I gave the Regent College Graduation Address in May I used this escapade as my opening illustration for 'The Crime of Living Life Too Cautiously'.

I wrote an exhortation to myself: 'Because you've had a heart attack, don't commit the crime of living life too cautiously.' It is a natural tendency to do so after a serious illness, or setback in business, or a breakdown in relationships. When we are hurt, in whatever manner, we tend to retreat inwards. I noted that Luci acknowledged there is a place for caution, especially where the security and welfare of others is concerned. Ask any debt counsellor, or person who has rushed into an unwise relationship and is living with the consequences. Yet we must avoid the crime of a life lived too cautiously.

Luci's words had been the ones I needed for launching Christina Press, for getting back into the flow of life, for making a fresh start.

I told myself Sir Christopher Wren would never have built St Paul's Cathedral if he had lived too cautiously and medical science would similarly have been hindered; Mount Everest would have remained unconquered; Sir Francis Chichester, with terminal lung cancer, would have buried his ambition to be the first sailor to single-handedly circumnavigate the world.

Cautious voices would have prevented George Muller from embarking on his venture of faith in Bristol, building orphanages, feeding 2,000 children, never telling anyone except God of his financial needs and showing to the world that 'our God and Father is the same faithful God as ever he was; as willing as ever to prove himself to be the living God, in our day as formerly'.

If he had committed the crime of living life too cautiously, Dr James Hudson Taylor would not have founded the China Inland Mission, now known as OMF International. 'When will it dawn on the Lord's people,' he asked, 'that God's commandment to preach the gospel to every creature was not intended for the wastepaper basket?'

Without risk on the part of the early Christians, the gospel would not have spread so rapidly; the good news would not have blazed its way around the world; the Apostle Paul might have opted for an administrative or teaching post in Jerusalem after one scary experience of shipwreck, one term of prolonged imprisonment.

Nearer home, as a newly qualified doctor, Ann would not have gone to Thailand, and I would not have voluntarily left the security of the Hodder boardroom in 1980 on my fiftieth birthday. As I once heard John Wimber say, 'Faith is spelt R I S K.'

In launching Christina Press, I accepted that God sometimes permits us to fail and during its first year there were anxious moments as expenditure exceeded income. Rather than have a bank overdraft we adjusted our planned output of new titles spreading them over a slightly longer period. In past years I had been fortunate enough to publish a score or more bestsellers; now I needed just one to transform our situation. I looked upwards for God's raven in the wilderness: it had never failed to appear before. It might be *Day by Day with God*.

But what if it wasn't forthcoming, if God didn't send it this time? Not because he didn't care but because he did. Could failure, like illness, be a gainful as well as a trying experience? Perhaps in my learning curve I was to be taught that disappointment takes us closer to God than achievement. 'We must go through many hardships to enter the kingdom of God' (Acts 14:22, NIV). From a prison in Rome the Apostle Paul wrote to the Philippians: 'Now I want you to know, brothers, that what has happened to me has really served to advance the gospel. As a result it has become clear throughout the whole palace guard and to everyone else that I am in chains for Christ. Because of my chains, most of the brothers in the Lord have been encouraged to speak the word of God more courageously and fearlessly' (Philippians 1:12–14, NIV). The church had prayed for Paul's release but for the present God wanted him under arrest. It was in prison that he wrote some of the epistles which are now our rich heritage.

Taking risks means facing our fears and involves the possibility of failure (as not taking them also does). Tournier says, 'We are always tempted to save what we have by refusing to put it at risk again. But this means the end of adventure.' Thomas Merton wrote, 'Do not be one of those who, rather than risk failure, never attempts anything.' And so my concluding lesson is:

Don't commit the crime of living life too cautiously.

The Twelfth Lesson

DON'T COMMIT THE CRIME OF LIVING LIFE TOO CAUTIOUSLY

As he walked by the Sea of Galilee, he saw two brothers, Simon who is called Peter and Andrew his brother, casting a net into the sea; for they were fishermen. And he said to them, 'Follow me, and I will make you fishers of men.' Immediately they left their nets and followed him. And going on from there he saw two other brothers, James the son of Zebedee and John his brother . . . and he called them. Immediately they left the boat and their father, and followed him.

—*Matthew 4:18–22 (RSV)*

After this he went out, and saw a tax collector, named Levi, sitting at the tax office; and he said to him, 'Follow me.' And he left everything, and rose and followed him.

—*Luke 2:27 (RSV)*

God's method in answering almost any prayer is the march-into-the-Red-Sea-and-it-divides method or march-right-up-to-the-walls-and-they-fall-down technique. You've got to have faith for that sort of venture and courage, too.

—*Peter Marshall*

A Final Word

During the last four years I have wished that we could choose the lessons that God teaches us, like selecting a course of study for a degree or an evening class. 'I want to be in your school, Lord, I really do, and, if I may, to choose my own syllabus. I have examined it carefully. I like parts of it very much. Please put me down for a series on coping with success, not with failure; for a course in growth and expansion, not limitation; for the Christian Olympics, not bodily weakness; for a Palm Sunday, not a Good Friday.'

'I am the teacher,' God replies. 'I choose the lessons, you have the choice of how you respond to them. Negatively or positively.'

So in his great training institute God speaks to us through our bodies, sometimes whispering, sometimes with a megaphone, telling us when to slow down, to take a break, to come to a halt. We may be foolish enough to think we do not need to change the pace for ourselves; then let us do so for our family and friends. Non-stop activity places an intolerable burden on those we love, frequently leading to stress and depression. Our caring heavenly Father desires us to live within the limits, to love ourselves and them enough to take a break. We are not indispensable – history demonstrates that – how swiftly we forget it.

He wants us as Christians to see our circumstances, those we love, and the world, with resurrection eyes; appreciating today as his gift, a special never-to-be-repeated moment in time.

So we live in a state of readiness for departure for, as Shelagh's death reminded us, while we do not know where his finger is on the clock of life, we know our times are in his hand. We journey, however, not as glum people, without hope, but as those who have most reason to celebrate, to have a party. We are the happiest people because 'it is not death to die'.

As I write this my cardiac consultant is considering, after yet another admission to hospital, whether I should be fitted with a pace-maker which would regulate the heart beat. Whether that will happen I doubt but on waking this morning I realise that pace-making is a major theme of my book. I scribble a prayer:

As I plan my day, the weeks ahead, and consider the appointments in my diary:
    Heavenly Father, be my pace-maker.
As the demands of life thrust themselves upon me, the duties, the responsibilities from which I should not hide:
    Heavenly Father, be my pace-maker.
When I am sometimes frail, unable to cope with people's expectations:
    Heavenly Father, be my pace-maker.
When my urge is to respond to any challenge, still me and be my peace.
Show me what I should and shouldn't do.
When I run ahead of you, or drop behind, bring me into step, that I may rest my tent where yours is.
God of action, God of stillness, God of peace; who asks us to bear our burdens and to lay them down, activate and de-activate me, that I may respond only to your command.

When the hardest thing is to pause when I wish to press ahead, to accept your rhythm when I see constant opportunities, may my heart beat be in time with yours.

Heavenly Father, be my pace-maker.

The Lessons From a Busy Life

The First Lesson	God speaks to us through our bodies
The Second Lesson	Learning to stop is the first step on the road back to sanity
The Third Lesson	I am not indispensable
The Fourth Lesson	Be ready for departure
The Fifth Lesson	Don't cling to the past
The Sixth Lesson	Live within the limits
The Seventh Lesson	Appreciate today
The Eighth Lesson	There is more to life than increasing its speed
The Ninth Lesson	Love yourself enough to take a break
The Tenth Lesson	It is not death to die
The Eleventh Lesson	See the world with resurrection eyes
The Twelfth Lesson	Don't commit the crime of living life too cautiously

Bibliography

de Caussade, Jean-Pierre, *Sacrament of the Present Moment* (Harper Collins, 1989).

Eddison, John, *The Last Lap* (Kingsway, 1986).

Fraser, Keath, *Worst Journeys* (Picador, 1991).

Foster, Richard, *Celebration of Discipline* (Hodder and Stoughton, 1980).

Graham, Billy, *Just as I Am* (Harper Collins, 1995).

Lloyd-Jones, Martyn, *Spiritual Depression* (Pickering and Inglis, 1965).

MacDonald, Gordon, *Ordering Your Private World* (Highland, 1985).

Parsons, Rob, *The Sixty Minute Father* (Hodder and Stoughton, 1995).

Pearson, Althea, *Growing through Loss and Grief* (Harper Collins, 1994).

Runcorn, David, *Space for God* (Darton, Longman and Todd, 1990).

Sanders, J.O., *Heaven, Better by Far* (Highland 1993).

Shaw, Luci, *Life Path* (Christina Press, 1997).

Spurgeon, C.H., *Lectures to My Students* (Passmore and Alabaster, 1890).

Smith, Anthony M., *Gateway to Life* (IVP, 1994).

Tournier, Paul, *The Adventure of Living* (Highland, 1983).

A Place for You (Highland, 1984).
Creative Suffering (SCM Press, 1982).
Webster, Jack, *Alistair MacLean* (Chapmans Publishers, 1991).

Further copies
of this book can be obtained
from your local Christian bookseller.
In case of difficulty by post
(phone 01892 663650)